BRITISH
COLUMBIA

I0797747

REEF

GALÁPAGOS

CALIFORNIA

Hawaii

AMAZON
RAINFOREST

DEAD SEA

ANTARCTICA
ANTARCTICA

GONE
FOREVER?

Question, connect and take action to become better citizens with a brighter future. Now that's smart thinking!

Gone Forever?

Places to See (and Save) Before They Disappear

ERIN SILVER

ILLUSTRATED BY

XULIN WANG

ORCA BOOK PUBLISHERS

Published in Canada and the United States in 2026 by Orca Book Publishers.

Library and Archives Canada Cataloguing in Publication
Title: Gone forever? : places to see (and save) before they disappear / Erin Silver ; illustrated by Xulin Wang.
Names: Silver, Erin, 1980- author | Xulin, illustrator
Series: Orca think ; 20.
Description: Series statement: Orca think ; 20 | Includes bibliographical references and index.
Identifiers: Canadiana (print) 20250155532 | Canadiana (ebook) 20250155540 |
ISBN 9781459840980 (hardcover) | ISBN 9781459840997 (PDF) | ISBN 9781459841000 (EPUB)
Subjects: LCSH: Global environmental change—Juvenile literature. | LCSH: Climatic changes—Juvenile literature. | LCSH: Environmental degradation—Juvenile literature.
Classification: LCC GE149 .S54 2026 | DDC j363.7—dc23

Library of Congress Control Number: 2025933020

Summary: Part of the nonfiction Orca Think series for middle-grade readers, this illustrated book introduces young people to places around the world that could disappear because of the effects of human-caused climate change.

Orca Book Publishers is committed to reducing the consumption of nonrenewable resources in the production of our books. We make every effort to use materials that support a sustainable future.

Orca Book Publishers gratefully acknowledges the support for its publishing programs provided by the following agencies: the Government of Canada, the Canada Council for the Arts and the Province of British Columbia through the BC Arts Council and the Book Publishing Tax Credit.

Cover and interior artwork by Xulin Wang.
Design by Troy Cunningham.
Edited by Maria Birmingham.

Printed and bound in South Korea.

29 28 27 26 • 1 2 3 4

CERTIFIED CANADIAN PUBLISHER

ORCA BOOK PUBLISHERS
orcabook.com

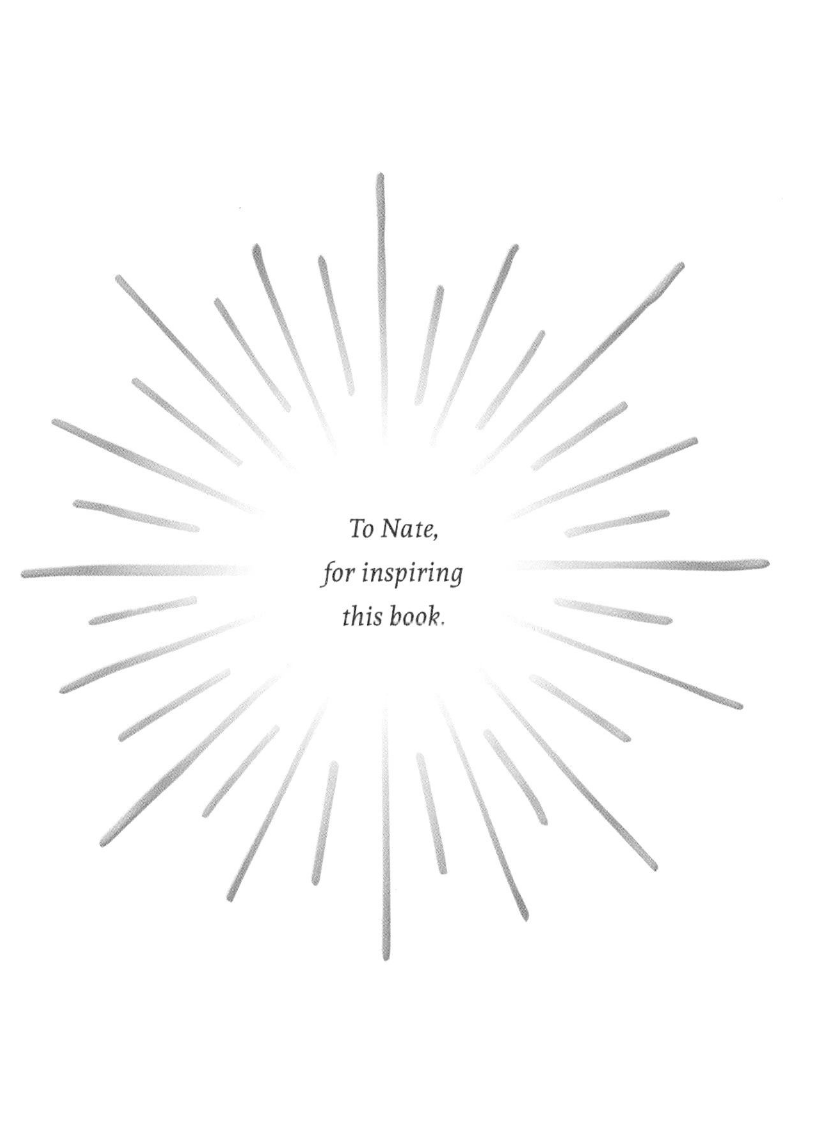

To Nate,
for inspiring
this book.

CONTENTS

INTRODUCTION:
GONE FOR GOOD. UNLESS... 1

CHAPTER ONE:
MAJOR MELTDOWN 5

- DESTINATION: ANTARCTICA 5
- TURNING UP THE HEAT 7
- UNDER THE SEA 9
- DESTINATION: THE ARCTIC 10
- MEET A POLAR BEAR EXPERT 12
- MELTING IMPACTS YOU 14
- IN DEPTH: POLLUTION AND THE POLES 14
- SKIING WITHOUT SNOW 16
- BEING "PRO" ACTIVE 18
- CONNECTING THROUGH ART: Q&A WITH AN ADVENTURE ARTIST 19
- EXPERIMENTING WITH SCIENCE 20

CHAPTER TWO:
CUE THE WATERWORKS 23

- DESTINATION: THE PACIFIC REGION 24
- STORM SURGES IN AUSTRALIA 25
- INDONESIA AND THE TRIPLE THREAT 26
- ON THE MOVE: CLIMATE MIGRANTS 27
- PLANNING FOR THE FUTURE: SOLUTIONS AROUND THE WORLD 27
- MEET A REBUILDING EXPERT 29
- GREENER PARKS 30
- INNOVATIVE SOLUTIONS TO FLOODING: Q&A WITH A CLIMATE ARCHITECT 31
- HOMES THAT FLOAT INSTEAD OF FLOOD 32
- EDUCATION IN ACTION 32
- DRY AS A DESERT: DEALING WITH DROUGHT 34
- IN DEPTH: KEEPING THE DEAD SEA ALIVE 36

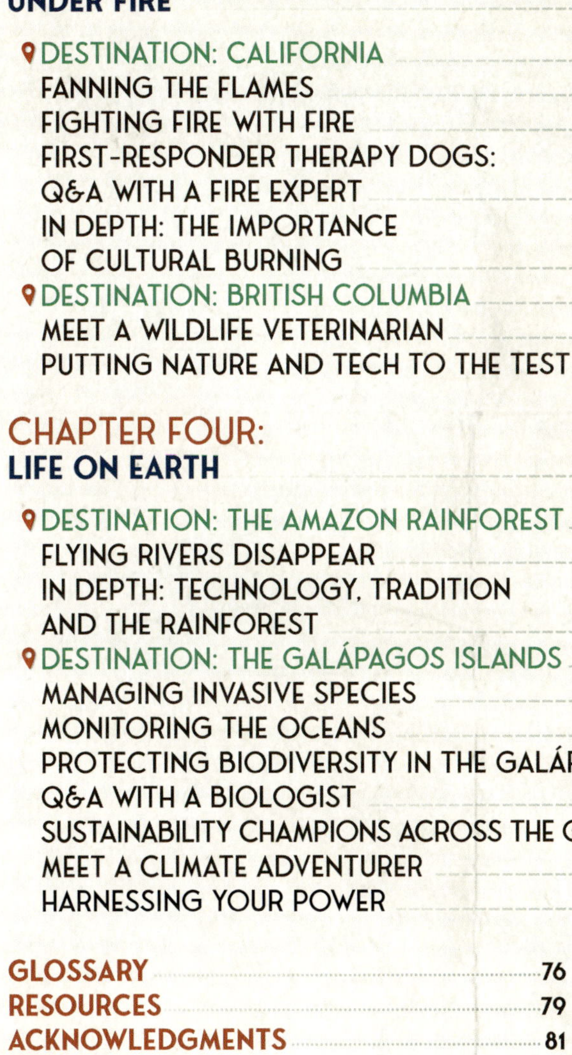

CHAPTER THREE:

UNDER FIRE 39

DESTINATION: CALIFORNIA 39
FANNING THE FLAMES 41
FIGHTING FIRE WITH FIRE 42
FIRST-RESPONDER THERAPY DOGS: Q&A WITH A FIRE EXPERT 43
IN DEPTH: THE IMPORTANCE OF CULTURAL BURNING 44
DESTINATION: BRITISH COLUMBIA 46
MEET A WILDLIFE VETERINARIAN 48
PUTTING NATURE AND TECH TO THE TEST 50

CHAPTER FOUR:

LIFE ON EARTH 55

DESTINATION: THE AMAZON RAINFOREST 55
FLYING RIVERS DISAPPEAR 58
IN DEPTH: TECHNOLOGY, TRADITION AND THE RAINFOREST 60
DESTINATION: THE GALÁPAGOS ISLANDS 62
MANAGING INVASIVE SPECIES 62
MONITORING THE OCEANS 63
PROTECTING BIODIVERSITY IN THE GALÁPAGOS: Q&A WITH A BIOLOGIST 65
SUSTAINABILITY CHAMPIONS ACROSS THE GLOBE 66
MEET A CLIMATE ADVENTURER 68
HARNESSING YOUR POWER 70

GLOSSARY 76
RESOURCES 79
ACKNOWLEDGMENTS 81
INDEX 83

GONE FOREVER?

INTRODUCTION

GONE FOR GOOD. UNLESS...

My young friend Nate called me one afternoon. That day in his geography class, he'd learned that many places around the world are disappearing because humans are impacting the climate and making Earth warmer. Nate was worried that these places will have sunk, shrunk, melted, burned or been depleted before he's able to see them with his own eyes. And that's a scary thought. Nate really wants to float in the Dead Sea, snorkel in the Great Barrier Reef and see penguins in the Arctic when he's older. So I started to do some research...

It turns out modern activities like driving, flying, operating factories and heating our homes have cost the planet. These everyday practices have released so many heat-trapping ***greenhouse gases*** into the air that climate scientists say Earth's average temperature has risen about 1.9°F (1.1°C) since 1880. While a few degrees might not sound like a lot, this increase has already been enough to cause all sorts of changes, including more heat waves, fires, severe storms, drought, flooding and melting of ***glaciers*** than ever before.

Gone Forever? takes readers on a trip around the world to discover how climate change is impacting countries around the globe.
BUENA VISTA IMAGES/GETTY IMAGES

All of this is negatively affecting people and wildlife and altering the world as we know it.

This is called ***climate change***, a term for significant long-term changes in Earth's temperatures and weather patterns. In the last 50 years alone, the temperature has increased faster than at any other time in our planet's history. NASA predicts that Earth's temperature could warm by 2.7°F (1.5°C) by 2050 and as much as 7.2°F (4°C) by the year 2100. This increase could be catastrophic.

But there is hope. Many environmental scientists say that if we make positive changes now, we can reduce our impact on the planet. Ready to find out more? Grab your suitcase for a tour of some of the incredible places at risk of disappearing due to climate change and find out how people are trying to keep that from happening. By learning more about our fascinating planet, I hope you'll be inspired to take climate action—readers like you are a big part of the solution. After all, the Dead Sea is pretty cool, and penguins are very cute, and I'd love to see them too!

THE ARCTIC

ONE
MAJOR MELTDOWN

Global warming is causing many of the world's glaciers and ***ice caps*** to melt. Though they may seem remote and not something we need to worry about, melting glaciers affect everyone, including me and you in our own homes. Surprising, right? To find out more, let's bundle up for a trek to some of Earth's chilliest areas.

DESTINATION: ANTARCTICA

Travel as far south as you can and you'll end up in the Antarctic. Bigger than all of Europe, Antarctica is a remote, ice-covered continent often described as the most beautiful place in the world. It's also the windiest and the coldest. Can you imagine being whipped by winds gusting up to 190 miles (300 kilometers) per hour or going outside in temperatures that can reach -144°F (-98°C)? Brrr! While it's definitely too cold for humans to live there year-round, the area is home to such wildlife as penguins, dolphins, whales and seals.

Playing in the snow is fun! Some places are colder and get more snow than others. Climate change means that places that should be cold are slowly warming up.

IMGORTHAND/GETTY IMAGES

Antarctica also contains 90 percent of the world's ice and 70 percent of the planet's fresh water. That means a lot of people around the world depend on its glaciers for food, water and even electricity. Antarctica is such an important natural laboratory that each year about 5,000 scientists stay in specially constructed research stations to study the surroundings. They've seen firsthand how the continent is being impacted by climate change.

PASSPORT TO MORE: Packing for Antarctica

An organization called Antarctic and Southern Ocean Coalition polled its researchers to find out what they pack when they visit Antarctica. Here are a few things they never go without:

- Warm clothes like waterproof pants, long underwear and socks.
- Bright-colored jackets—especially red ones so they can more easily see each other in whiteouts or other harsh conditions.
- Sunglasses and sunscreen—the sun's reflection off the ice is very bright.
- Lots of chocolate—even scientists have a sweet tooth!

TURNING UP THE HEAT

About 90 percent of Antarctica's glaciers have shrunk since the 1960s. It's no wonder—scientists say that global warming has caused temperatures in the Antarctic to increase at five times the global average. Temperatures there have risen by about 6°F (3.3°C) since the 1940s. If you think six degrees doesn't sound too bad, consider this: it's the difference between a snowman and a puddle of water! And slight increases in the temperature in the Antarctic set off a chain reaction around the world.

THE INFO EXPRESS

Yes, you can visit Antarctica! About 30,000 tourists go there each year. Their trips are carefully managed to make sure the continent isn't damaged by pollution from boats or garbage left behind.

Antarctica is an amazing place to visit, inspiring everyone from artists to scientists with its majestic beauty. But this landscape is changing.

CONNECT IMAGES/BRETT PHIBBS/GETTY IMAGES

Antarctica plays a special role in maintaining the world's climate. When it warms up, consequences are felt around the world.

PAUL SOUDERS/GETTY IMAGES

THE WORLD'S THERMOSTAT

Antarctica helps regulate the global climate, kind of like a thermostat balances the temperature in a home. Here are some ways it's important:

- Its ***ice sheets*** reflect sun away from the Earth, keeping the planet cooler.
- Ice works like a dam, freezing so much water that it prevents coastal areas all over the world from flooding. In fact, if all the ice on Antarctica were to melt, the oceans would rise by 200 feet (60 meters), putting places like Florida, Denmark and Bangladesh underwater.
- Antarctica's permafrost (frozen rock or soil) keeps ***carbon dioxide*** locked up as if in a vault. As permafrost melts, carbon is released into the air, worsening climate change.
- Antarctica is surrounded by the Southern Ocean. Its currents work like a conveyor belt, circulating water around the world—similar to how luggage moves on a carousel at the airport. When ice melts, currents are disrupted, and the rest of the world gets more extreme weather systems like cyclones, tornadoes and hurricanes.

UNDER THE SEA

The oceans play a key role in regulating climate change and maintaining ***ecosystems***. But climate change is impacting the oceans too. If we take a deep dive into Antarctica's Southern Ocean, we see how. Take phytoplankton, for example. These microscopic plants absorb huge amounts of carbon dioxide from the atmosphere during ***photosynthesis***. In that process they release ***oxygen***, which is why oceans are often called the lungs of the planet. Over the last 25 years, scientists have found that phytoplankton in the Southern Ocean have started to grow later than normal and they stop growing sooner. Smaller blooms mean less carbon is taken from the air. That's bad news for the planet, as well as for the krill that feed on the plants.

KRILL TO THE RESCUE

Krill are small, shrimp-like crustaceans. Measuring about the length of a paper clip, krill eat phytoplankton. Then they poop out pellets that drop to the ocean floor. Since the pellets are filled with carbon, iron and other nutrients, krill help fertilize the ocean floor and keep carbon out of the air. In fact, scientists have discovered that krill can remove up to 13 billion tons (12 billion metric tons) of carbon from Earth's atmosphere each year—about the same as what's produced by 35 million cars each year! When climate change causes phytoplankton blooms to shrink, krill have less to eat. With fewer krill, less carbon is locked away.

Krill are like an all-you-can-eat buffet for ocean life. In a single day, a blue whale can eat 6 tons (5.4 metric tons) of krill. Meanwhile, Adélie and chinstrap penguins get almost all of their calories from krill. August 11 is World Krill Day—a day to celebrate krill's role in fighting climate change and keeping the entire Antarctic ecosystem healthy.

The Yup'ik People living in the Far North have so much experience managing harsh climates that they came up with an invention to shield their eyes from the blinding sun as it bounces off the snowy landscape: snow goggles!

JULIAN IDROBO/WIKIMEDIA COMMONS/ CC BY-SA 2.0

DESTINATION: THE ARCTIC

Right on top of the world, above an imaginary ring called the Arctic Circle, lies the Arctic. More livable than Antarctica, the average temperature on a winter day is -40°F (-40°C). The summer has average temperatures of 50°F (10°C). About four million people live in the Arctic, which includes parts of Canada, Russia, the United States, Greenland, Sweden, Norway, Iceland and Finland. Indigenous Peoples have called the Arctic home for thousands of years. They have developed incredible ways to adapt to life in this frozen, snow-covered landscape. For instance, the Yup'ik invented snow goggles, made of antlers, ivory or wood to shield their eyes from the blinding sunlight that bounces off the snowy landscape. (What a bright idea!) The Arctic is also home to a range of wildlife, including polar bears, whales and smaller species such as Arctic fox and salmon.

BREAKING THE ICE

The Arctic's ice caps, ice sheets and glaciers hold about 10 percent of the world's fresh water. Just like the Antarctic, this polar region's frozen surface reflects sunlight, keeping temperatures cool and stabilizing the world's climate. Climate change has caused the Arctic to warm, and it's happening two to three times faster than the global average. In the last 40 years, global warming has reduced year-round sea ice levels by 40 percent. This is having an impact on humans, as well as wildlife, the economy and the environment.

SOMETHING FISHY

One of the areas in which climate change is making its mark in the Arctic is the salmon population. The Yukon River has been closed to salmon fishing for several years. Warmer water temperatures caused by climate change have made it harder for salmon to grow and survive. Fisheries in the Arctic, which supply restaurants and stores all over the world with wild-caught salmon, are struggling. And that's not the only issue. Salmon are a keystone species. That means they provide nutrition for many other living things, from land animals like wolves and bears to birds like eagles and even marine mammals like orca. With fewer salmon, there's less food to go around. The decline also affects people in the region—including those in Arctic Indigenous communities—who will need to rely more and more on other foods in the future. Many foods are transported in from long distances and have significant costs attached to them. Adapting to climate change is important to ***food security***, especially because options like salmon are becoming scarce. Unfortunately, adapting is not always easy.

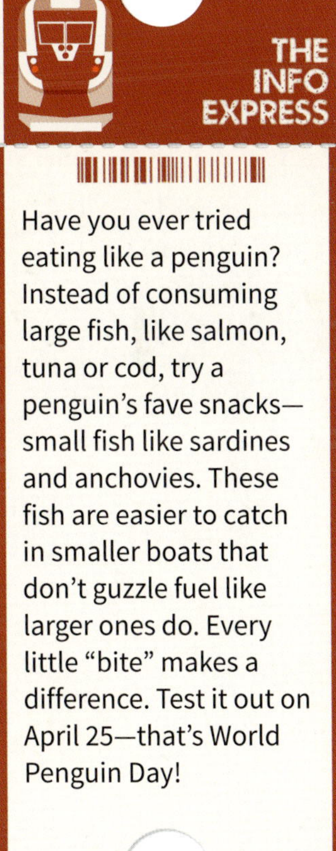

Have you ever tried eating like a penguin? Instead of consuming large fish, like salmon, tuna or cod, try a penguin's fave snacks—small fish like sardines and anchovies. These fish are easier to catch in smaller boats that don't guzzle fuel like larger ones do. Every little "bite" makes a difference. Test it out on April 25—that's World Penguin Day!

PASSPORT TO MORE:
The *Exxon Valdez* Oil Spill

In March 1989, 11 million gallons (about 41 million liters) of crude oil accidentally spilled from a ship in Alaska, covering coastlines and killing hundreds of thousands of seabirds, otters, seals and whales. As well, the Indigenous communities who lived along the coast were profoundly impacted by the devastation of an essential food source. The *Exxon Valdez* oil spill was infamous for being the worst oil spill in US history…until the next one in 2010.

FOOL'S GOLD

And there's more. Some areas in the Arctic region contain valuable minerals like gold, copper and coal, plus oil and natural gas deposits. As climate change causes the ice to melt, the Arctic becomes more accessible to mining and drilling companies—many of which are fighting over who gets what. This is commonly being done without considerations for the Indigenous Peoples who they wish to displace and whose land the companies wish to exploit. Experts agree that mining and drilling would destroy salmon habitats—and the communities and ecosystems that depend on them—and create billions of tons of toxic waste. Many Indigenous communities and some environmentalists are trying to keep these companies out of the Arctic to preserve this important part of the world.

MEET A POLAR BEAR EXPERT

Erica Jacques loves her job as wildlife care keeper in the Arctic tundra section of the Toronto Zoo. Every day she works with animals found in the Arctic. While she likes feeding, training and caring for all of the Canadian Arctic animals, including the fox and caribou, the polar bears are Jacques's favorite.

"Polar bears are so fascinating," says Jacques. "As a species, they have adapted so well to the cold climate. For example, polar bears, which are the world's largest land ***carnivore***, have hollow hairs that trap warm air against their bodies, as well as small ears to avoid frostbite. While polar bears know how to swim, they try to avoid it to conserve energy. When they need to eat, these bears, which each can weigh about as much as nine men, have a special way of getting their meals. It's called 'still hunting.' Polar bears either find a hole in the ice or they make a hole with their massive paws. They lie in wait for a seal

It's not just people that are affected by climate change. When cold places like the Arctic get warmer, animals such as polar bears can't survive. Now their populations are at risk.
COURTESY OF THE TORONTO ZOO

to come up for a breath. They have to be very still and patient. Then they grab it."

HUNTING FOR FOOD

Polar bears are one of the animals most threatened by global warming. "A polar bear's main food source is seals, but polar bears can only catch seals if there's solid ice over the water," Jacques explains. "Every year, with temperatures rising, the ice-forming season starts later and ends earlier. Over the last 30 years, they've lost four weeks of their hunting season."

In other words, without sea ice polar bears can't hunt for food. The bears are getting thinner, and mothers often can't feed their cubs, so fewer survive every year. Today polar bears are ***endangered***. The International Union for Conservation of Nature estimates that there are currently about 26,000 polar bears worldwide. If sea ice continues to melt at its current rate, we could lose all but a few polar bear populations by 2100.

That's made Jacques and partners like Polar Bears International and World Wildlife Fund more determined than ever to raise awareness about climate change and find ways to work together to conserve the Arctic habitat.

MELTING IMPACTS YOU

International researchers in a Canadian study recently analyzed data from 440,000 satellite images and found that more than half the world's glaciers are expected to disappear within 80 years. Even if you can't see a glacier from your window, its melting affects all of us. How so? Let's take rice as an example. Rice is a staple of many diets. Depending on where you live, the rice you eat may come from Asia's Himalayan mountain glaciers. In fact, about one-third of the world's rice is grown in this mountain range, which spans countries including India, China and Pakistan. It takes a lot of water to grow rice, and about 130 million farmers depend on the ***meltwater*** from the Himalayan glaciers to grow it. Experts say more than half these glaciers will have melted completely by 2100, which means there won't be enough meltwater to grow rice and other crops like corn, wheat, and other fruits and vegetables. A water shortage would have a major impact on the food supply for billions of people. That's why researchers are looking at ways to make sure there's enough food to go around in the future. For instance, they're changing how water is stored, altering farming methods and focusing on growing food we can eat rather than crops for other purposes, such as cotton for making clothing.

Alison Criscitiello loves going on research expeditions to the Arctic. It's a great place to study climate change and learn more about how the world is connected by the impacts of climate change.
REBECCA HASPEL

IN DEPTH: POLLUTION AND THE POLES

Alison Criscitiello is an American ice-core scientist and an expert on glaciers. Every spring, she travels to remote places in the Arctic to drill out cylinders of ice, called ice cores. She studies this ice to look for any traces of chemicals used in past decades. This helps her better understand how humans have impacted and polluted the planet.

Criscitiello is one of the few ***glaciologists*** in the world using ice cores to understand which pollutants were transported to the Arctic through the air and ended up in the ice. "These pollutants affect the health of local communities, fish and wildlife," she explains.

No matter where we live, we're all directly connected to what's happening at the poles. "Water cycles around the globe through currents," Criscitiello says. "I live in Edmonton, Alberta—about 250 miles (more than 400 kilometers) from the Columbia Icefield in the Canadian Rockies—but ***water towers*** connect those glaciers to water that comes out of our taps. If the ice is contaminated, and global warming causes it to melt, those contaminants will ultimately come back to us in our drinking water."

Her ice-core research has found that contaminants banned years ago have accumulated in various parts of our frozen planet and now are melting into our water supply. Criscitiello is also finding ***microplastics*** in glaciers from products like plastic toys and single-use bottles, as well as tiny particles from the nonstick coating in frying pans, and all of this is cycling back into our water supply. "With melting glaciers, pollutants in our snow and ice are coming back to haunt us," Criscitiello says.

To stop glaciers from melting entirely, the world needs to ensure that the average global temperature doesn't increase by more than 3°F (1.5°C) by 2050. Criscitiello thinks we can do it. She has a lot of faith in young people today. That's why she co-created a program called Girls on Ice Canada. The program takes teen girls on expedition to see glaciers and learn about science and the natural world. "I hope it will spark in them the desire to be agents of change in their own communities."

Alison Criscitiello believes that by bringing girls with her through the Girls on Ice Canada program, even more people can learn how climate change is affecting the planet.
REBECCA HASPEL

HELPING OUT AT HOME

There are things you and I can do every day to help combat climate change.

- Reduce your use of plastics. Plastic products break down into tiny particles that can get blown away in the wind. Other chemicals attach themselves to these particles and can hitchhike all the way to the Arctic and its ice.
- Stop using nonstick cookware. It produces chemical compounds that don't break down in the environment. Talk to the adults in your life about choosing stainless steel, cast iron or ceramic instead.
- Get outside. Criscitiello explains, "Even just taking up an outdoor sport gives people personal experiences with nature, and that makes us better advocates for it. People protect the things they love."
- Be involved. Some students organize climate marches, while others might champion an eco club at school. Others make simple changes at home. Learn about the issues, get involved, and show leaders that the environment matters to you.

SKIING WITHOUT SNOW

Warmer weather doesn't just impact far-off glaciers. It affects mountains near you too. For the millions of recreational skiers, snowboarders and snowshoers around the world, that may be hard to hear.

Research shows that in Aspen, Colorado—a haven for winter-sports enthusiasts—the ski season is a month shorter than it was 40 years ago. In the future some resorts might not get enough snow to have a ski season at all. Meanwhile, in Ottawa, the Rideau Canal Skateway—the world's largest naturally frozen ice rink—couldn't open in 2023 for the first time in its history. Temperatures were too mild for the canal to freeze over.

OLYMPIC NIGHTMARE

Disappearing winters are a big problem for winter Olympians too. An international team of scientists found that if carbon emissions keep increasing at the current rate, by 2080 Sapporo, Japan, will be the only former Olympic city with suitable snow conditions to host the winter games. Previous host cities, including Beijing, PyeongChang and Calgary, will no longer be options. Already athletes are complaining that snow in these places is too slushy or icy.

It's causing skiers to crash and get injured. Because global warming means seasons are unpredictable, some winters might get too much snow, and athletes could see other unsafe conditions—like avalanches—instead. That's led organizations like the International Olympic Committee (IOC) to take action. It is making changes to reduce the ***carbon footprint*** of the Olympic Games by doing things like reducing transportation emissions and producing less waste.

BEING "PRO" ACTIVE

Elladj Baldé is a Canadian former competitive figure skater whose career really took flight when videos of his backflips while skating—filmed on majestic frozen lakes in the Canadian Rockies—went viral on social media. Baldé says he can absolutely see the effects that our warming climate has had on our winter environments. "Glaciers are melting and disappearing, and the wild ice season is shortening, becoming more difficult to predict."

As a climate activist and ambassador for an organization called Protect Our Winters, Baldé is helping raise awareness for climate change. "Through my figure skating, I work to motivate my audience to fall in love with the winter and take action in any way they can, big or small. I believe that each step we take makes a difference."

Elladj Baldé believes that his figure-skating videos could help other people fall in love with the natural beauty of winter and take action to protect it.

PAUL ZIZKA

CONNECTING THROUGH ART: Q&A WITH AN ADVENTURE ARTIST

Expedition and adventure artist Colin Parker combines his passion for art with a love for exploring remote landscapes. Based in England, Parker has traveled all over the world and hopes his digital drawings will inspire viewers to protect remote and fragile environments. The landscape that sparks his creativity the most is the Arctic.

COLIN PARKER

Q: HOW DID YOU END UP WORKING IN THIS FIELD?

A: My journey to become an expedition and adventure artist was rooted in my love for creating art and my strong connection to the wild and remote wilderness. It's a way for me to share the beauty and awe of the world's most remote and untouched places through my unique perspective...I feel more at home under a starry sky than any roof and four walls!

Q: WHAT'S IT LIKE DRAWING IN THE ARCTIC?

A: When I first went to the Arctic, the biting cold was an unwavering adversary. We had to adapt to various sleeping arrangements. From seeking natural shelters to digging "snow graves" for protection against the elements, each method demanded resourcefulness and resilience...Also, traditional art supplies became impractical, so I draw [now] with my digital drawing tablet. It lets me capture the Arctic's beauty without lugging around bulky materials, dealing with frozen paint and having to wash brushes. I also learned to use my stylus with gloves on so my fingers don't freeze!

Q: HOW DOES ART HELP CONSERVATION AND SUSTAINABILITY?

A: Art has the power to touch the heart and soul. It's not merely about showing people these places; it's about transporting them there emotionally. My art allows individuals to see what I saw and to feel the profound connection to these endangered landscapes. I hope my art highlights the urgent need to protect these fragile environments for generations to come.

Researchers have lots of cool ideas for how they can protect glaciers from melting, many of which involve cutting-edge science but are very expensive. In the future, some of their ideas may become a reality.
ROBERTHARDING/ALAMY STOCK PHOTO

EXPERIMENTING WITH SCIENCE

The science community is experimenting with several exciting ideas to stop glaciers from melting altogether. Massive ***geoengineering*** projects would cost billions of dollars, but they could buy us a few centuries of time to deal with global warming.

- Some ski resorts in Italy and the Swiss Alps are using reflective blankets called geotextiles to reflect sun away from the mountains so the snow doesn't melt as quickly. While this technology may be great for smaller glaciers, the blankets are expensive to produce, and it would take teams of people several months to cover an entire mountain range. Thus experts say this idea may not be a long-term solution to stop glaciers from melting.

- Scientists at the University of Arizona have suggested collecting water from underneath glaciers through pumps powered by wind. Then they would spray the seawater on top of certain sections of melting glaciers to encourage ice growth. These scientists say that adding layers of ice to the average glacier would be like "instantaneously setting back the clock about seventeen years."

- Scientists involved in the Arctic Ice Project are researching an innovative idea. They propose spreading a thin layer of reflective glass beads over certain small regions of the Arctic to stop ice from melting during the summer, thereby allowing glaciers to remain frozen throughout the year. They believe this could stabilize the climate for 15 years, giving the world time to ***decarbonize*** or find ways to rely less on energy sources that pollute the planet.

PASSPORT TO MORE: It All Comes Out in the Wash

When plastic bottles are dumped, and when our ***synthetic*** clothes are washed, they eventually become microplastics in our oceans. They stay there for hundreds of years. Add oil spills, discarded fishing nets and flaking paint from ships into the mix, and it's a recipe for disaster. Plastic kills over a million seabirds each year and more than 100,000 marine mammals. And chemical pollution from things like fertilizer runoff is so bad in some sections of the ocean that little can survive there. These areas are called ***dead zones***.

PACIFIC
ISLANDS

TWO
CUE THE WATERWORKS

Imagine filling up your bathtub with water, then letting the tap run...and run...and run. Before long the whole bathroom would be flooded. That's kind of what's happening on our planet. Warmer temperatures are causing sea levels to rise, partly because of melting glaciers. Since 1880 global average sea levels have risen by more than 8 inches (20 centimeters). Experts estimate that by the year 2100 levels will increase by another 4 feet (1.2 meters). Global warming also changes weather patterns, causing more rain and severe storms. This causes flooding in some cities. Flooding is an especially big problem in areas that are already sinking into the ground because of the way the city was built or is being managed. Meanwhile, in other places, the opposite is happening. Water is evaporating, and there isn't enough to go around. In this chapter, we'll head around the world to visit places that are flooding, sinking and shrinking.

Flooding has become a problem in places around the world, so it's important to gear up and have a good pair of rain boots. There are many ways people are preparing for too much water.

AIRE IMAGES/GETTY IMAGES

DESTINATION: THE PACIFIC REGION

Known for their beauty and remoteness, the Pacific Islands are teeming with wildlife, beaches and culture. But the threats posed by climate change are very real in these islands. Many are in danger of being swallowed by water and disappearing. And islanders have been trying to warn the world since the 1980s. Kiribati—the populated area that experiences New Year's Day first each year—may be the first to drown. The sea level has risen 2 to 4 inches (5 to 11 centimeters) over the past 30 years—faster than the global average. Kiribati is at risk of having its coastlines, homes and economy washed away by water. Other low-lying islands like the Maldives, Vanuatu and Fiji are also expected to vanish in the coming decades. It seems unfair that these small countries emit the least amount of carbon but are hugely impacted by the countries that emit the most.

STORM SURGES IN AUSTRALIA

Just as small Pacific islands are being impacted, large continents in the Pacific are feeling the effects of climate change too. That's because warmer oceans and air conditions caused by climate change are creating more frequent and violent storms. These storms bring higher tides, ***storm surges*** and so much extra rain to some places that roads, buildings and homes are swept away. Every year storms like this cause enough damage to force millions of people to evacuate their homes. As I was writing this chapter, Tropical Cyclone Jasper brought so much rain to Cairns, Australia—25.6 inches (65 centimeters) in just 19 hours—that the city was flooded in less than a day. Its infrastructure—things like roads, buildings and sewer systems—weren't equipped to handle so much water in such a short time. Some families were stranded overnight on rooftops until rescue teams could save them. Floodwaters rose so high that car doors couldn't be opened. A small plane sat partly submerged in water as though it were a boat, and an 8-foot (2.4-meter)-long crocodile was swept along by a flooded creek. The Australian government predicts that extreme rainfall events like Jasper will become more intense in some parts of the country, with rising sea levels flooding entire communities, even as other parts of Australia face extreme heat, drought and wildfires. (You'll read more about wildfires in chapter 3.)

PASSPORT TO MORE: The El Niño Effect

Every two to seven years, you hear more about a climate pattern called ***El Niño***. This recurring natural phenomenon causes the surface waters of the ***Equatorial Pacific Ocean*** to warm up, changing the speed and strength of sea currents. It's enough to spark extreme weather—from droughts, wildfires and heat waves in some places to deadly floods and severe storms in others. It affects weather and marine life worldwide. Researchers believe that climate change is strengthening the El Niño effect, which means we may see more record-breaking temperatures and catastrophic weather conditions in the future.

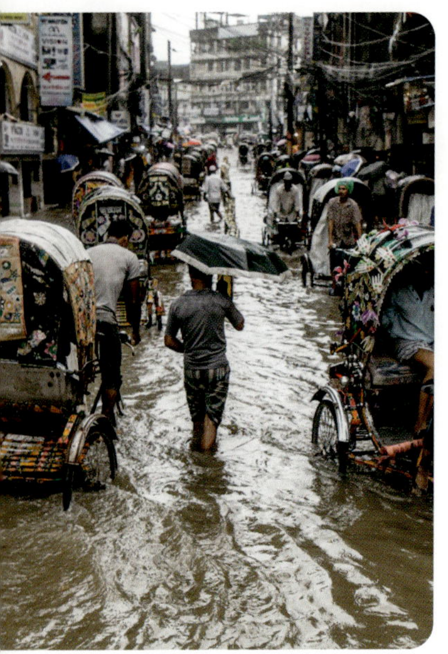

A combination of factors means that some places are sinking and flooding at the same time. It's such a problem in Indonesia that its capital city has to be moved elsewhere.

AMDADPHOTO/SHUTTERSTOCK.COM

INDONESIA AND THE TRIPLE THREAT

More than 10 million residents in Jakarta, the capital city of Indonesia, are facing a similar fate. Every five or six years, the densely packed city floods because of sea-level rise and increased storm activity. Not only that, the city is sinking, getting closer to sea level. In fact, Jakarta has one of the fastest rates of ***land subsidence*** (gradual or sudden sinking of the earth's surface) in the world. The combination of the city's weight and, especially, residents' pumping of groundwater has caused the ground to compact and sink. Each flooding event turns the city's streets into a mucky swimming pool, flooding buildings and contaminating the water supply.

Now Indonesia has decided to move its capital city to a spot 1,250 miles (2,000 kilometers) away, on the island of Borneo. It's expected to take decades to erect new buildings here, and there's already a ban on taking groundwater from beneath the city. Today, as Jakarta sinks, researchers have found that at least 33 other cities around the world are also sinking by about 0.3 inches (1 centimeter) a year. The fastest-sinking cities are in South and Southeast Asia.

PASSPORT TO MORE: Saving Endangered Species

Animals are impacted by climate change too. A rodent called Bramble Cay melomys, once found on an island near Australia, was the first mammal to become extinct because of climate change. Its entire population drowned after its habitat was destroyed by repeated flooding.

Today the world's largest lizard, the Komodo dragon, is also at risk of disappearing because its habitat is flooding too. There are only about 1,400 adults left in the wilderness of low-lying islands in Indonesia. Zoos, the Indonesian government and conservation groups are trying to ensure that the species survives. They are also helping other endangered animals, including orangutans, Sumatran tigers and Sumatran elephants.

ON THE MOVE: CLIMATE MIGRANTS

When cities don't or can't adapt to flooding, homes and businesses are wiped out, disease and poverty spread, and people have no choice but to move elsewhere. When people are forced to flee their homes because of climate change, it's called climate migration, and the people who flee are known as ***climate migrants***. Some experts say that by 2050, 1.2 billion people could have to move because of weather-related events, like flooding, brought on by climate change. Just imagine taking only the belongings you can carry to a completely new place where you have to rebuild your life from scratch.

Tokyo, Japan, is one of the rainiest cities in the world. But a giant underwater facility was recently built to divert rainwater. The successful facility is so big, a space rocket could fit inside it. If you ever make it to Japan, you can even take a tour!

PLANNING FOR THE FUTURE: SOLUTIONS AROUND THE WORLD

If climate change continues at its current pace, experts say that by the 2050s some cities will flood 5 to 10 times more often than they do today. More than 800 million people living in 570 cities around the world—including Miami, New York, Bangkok and Shanghai—will be impacted. Projects are underway, even in elementary schools, to figure out how to adapt to climate change and plan for the future. These plans are innovative, exciting and sometimes very simple.

MANAGING FLOODS WITH MANGROVES

As an effective and inexpensive way to fight flooding, several international organizations, including the World Bank and ActionAid, are planting and protecting mangrove forests in places hardest hit by climate change and flooding, including coastlines in Indonesia, Bangladesh, Kenya, Cambodia, India and the Philippines. Mangroves are woody trees that grow along shorelines and can thrive in salty soil. Their hardy underwater roots absorb water, and their thick, tangled branches act as a barrier against the impact of waves. Mangroves improve water quality and provide habitat for species from fish to birds to monkeys. Mangrove forests also absorb carbon.

ENGINEERING MARVEL

You've probably heard of Venice, Italy, famous for its gondolas, canals...and its flooding. Today, the average seawater level in Venice is at its highest because of sea-level rise, melting glaciers and sinking land. All these factors mean the city floods three or four times a year instead of once a decade as it did a century ago. Thankfully, an engineering marvel called MOSE (Modulo Sperimentale Elettromeccanico, or Experimental Electromechanical Module) is creating a fortress around the ancient city to stop it from flooding. Unlike other ***dams*** and ***dikes*** built to manage flooding in places like the Netherlands and Canada, MOSE is underwater during good weather. But when there's a storm surge and water levels rise, its 78 metal barriers emerge from the sea and keep the water away from the city. The dike system of five-story-high barriers took 30 years to plan, 20 years to build, and cost $6 billion. More research is being done to make sure this solution can stand up to climate change into the future.

Huge barrier systems have been designed and developed to deal with vast amounts of water flooding cities like Venice. The solution is working for now, but it might not always be the case.
CHICCODODIFC/GETTY IMAGES

MEET A REBUILDING EXPERT

Amy Chester is managing director of Rebuild by Design, an organization that has helped more than a dozen at-risk cities, including New York City and San Francisco, plan for problems caused by climate change. The organization is designing and implementing several exciting projects to help cities plan for the future. The idea of ***climate resilience***—the ability of cities to prepare for and live with climate change—is behind every project. "We don't want to lose our homes, jobs or our friends, and we don't want to have to move, so we plan ahead," says Chester. "We know climate change is coming—it's already here—so what are the steps we can take together to adapt in ways that have multiple benefits?"

Chester is excited about projects like these:

Amy Chester is an expert in climate resilience. She has many projects underway to help protect cities that are dealing with flooding. She gives lots of talks and helps experts manage too much water.

CAMERON BAYLOCK/
REBUILD BY DESIGN

PASSPORT TO MORE: The Big Easy and Hurricane Katrina

When Hurricane Katrina hit the United States in 2005, the city of New Orleans, Louisiana, was devastated. Its storm barriers failed, causing 80 percent of the city to flood and over $100 billion in damage. Worst of all, more than 1,300 people died. After Katrina, the US government built an expensive system of ***levees*** and ***floodgates*** around the city. These barriers were stronger and dug deeper into the ground. By the time Hurricane Ida arrived in 2021, New Orleans was ready—the new and improved barriers kept the city from flooding. Residents could rest easy once again.

GREENER PARKS

Parks like this one in Singapore are being built to manage flooding. They are designed to transfer water from one point to another through waterways, helping disperse and contain it.

PAGODASHOPHOUSE/WIKIMEDIA COMMONS/CC BY-SA 3.0

Parks aren't just for playing anymore—they can also keep communities safe. A giant park called Chulalongkorn University Centenary Park was built to face climate change head-on in Bangkok, Thailand. A city already at sea level, Bangkok is also threatened by sea-level rise, storm surges and lots of rain during monsoon season. In addition to providing running paths, bike lanes and open space for residents, the park can also hold up to 1 million gallons (3.7 million liters) of water in special tanks to prevent the city from flooding. That's more than the amount of water needed to fill an Olympic-sized swimming pool! Water that's collected during storms is treated and used to water the park during dry seasons.

And Singapore's Bishan-Ang Mo Kio Park might look like it's flooding, but that's the point. Since Singapore often floods, this park was designed with a canal that sends rainwater downstream to a network of drains in the city. The canal, which runs through the center of the park, can manage floods as high as 10 feet (3 meters).

INNOVATIVE SOLUTIONS TO FLOODING:
Q&A WITH A CLIMATE ARCHITECT

Denmark is surrounded by trouble. The sea level is rising around the Scandinavian country, and Danes face both extreme rain events and storm surges on the coast. When a devastating storm tore through Denmark in 2011, experts realized they needed to adapt to the new reality. Denmark has since become a leader in designing creative solutions to climate change. Flemming Rafn, an architect and cofounder of Tredje Natur (Third Nature) in Copenhagen, is part of this movement. He has helped find unique ways for cities to adapt to climate change—solutions like pop-up parking lots!

COURTESY OF FLEMMING RAFN

Q: HOW DO CLIMATE CHANGE AND ARCHITECTURE GO TOGETHER?

A: We often see the city and nature as opposites. Many of the problems we have today in cities, like too much heat, too much water and sad urban spaces, can be lessened if we learn from nature.

Q: HOW IMPORTANT IS ARCHITECTURE TO CLIMATE CHANGE?

A: Buildings and cities are the most resource-consuming things we can make on the planet, so a lot of the problems we face now are directly linked to the way we live. But if we...transform them to our new reality, we can continue to thrive even if it gets hotter and drier and we see more extreme weather.

Q: WHAT IS A POP-UP PARKING LOT, AND WHY SHOULD CITIES BUILD THEM?

A: Cities need space for nature, recreation, communities and exciting urban areas. They also need room for practical stuff like cars and bikes. And because of the new climate reality, we need new capacity for water—both for limiting extreme rain and flooding, but also because we see more heat and droughts in the summer. And to fit all this into dense cities like New York and Copenhagen, we designed a parking lot for cars and bikes underground. It's like a giant corkscrew that floats when we have extreme rain. It also stores water we can use when it's dry.

Elizabeth English works with students on programs to help people prevent their existing homes from flooding by adapting the houses to make them float when it rains. So far she has run programs in such places as Vietnam and Canada.
COURTESY OF ELIZABETH ENGLISH

HOMES THAT FLOAT INSTEAD OF FLOOD

Architects aren't stopping at floating parking lots. They have designed homes meant to rise above extreme flooding. Amphibious houses rest on the ground in dry conditions and float when nearby waterways flood. Baca Architects is a leader in aqua-tecture in London. They are designing affordable amphibious homes with bases that allow homes to rise as much as 8 feet (2.5 meters) in serious floods and float on the floodwater. In the future, the firm believes entire communities of floating homes will be built, making London better prepared for flooding and climate change.

RAISE THE ROOF

It's not just new homes that are being built to float. A nonprofit called the Buoyant Foundation Project is raising existing homes in flood-prone regions. Established by Professor Elizabeth English from the University of Waterloo in Ontario, her project involves retrofitting homes in Vietnam by adding floating blocks, poles and framing. "We need to be supporting the communities of people who have been living in the same place for generations and, in some cases, hundreds of years," says English. "They deserve to be able to stay in the place they love if they are able to stay there safely."

EDUCATION IN ACTION

Creative ideas are flowing at schools too. For example, teachers at Dodge Elementary School in Grand Island, Nebraska, challenged fifth graders to think about solutions to flooding during a recent science fair. The Flood Barrier Challenge tasked students with designing ways to prevent homes from being

flooded during storms. Students researched water-resistant materials, built flood barriers and tested their experiments at the fair. Their ideas were even featured on the local news.

Rain gardens absorb water during a flood and help drain excess water into the sewer system. This prevents areas like school parking lots and playgrounds from flooding. It's a cool and innovative way for students to learn firsthand about solutions to flooding.

JCHANNELL/SHUTTERSTOCK.COM

Mount Tabor Middle School in Portland, Oregon, turned an underused parking area into a rain garden. The garden funnels stormwater from the school roof, parking lot and playground to prevent the area's sewer system from flooding during major storms. The water is absorbed by plants, and the ground dries out within a day of a big storm. In addition to preventing floods, the garden also serves as an outdoor classroom where students learn about climate change and ways to manage floods.

DRY AS A DESERT: DEALING WITH DROUGHT

Climate experts believe that places already dealing with too much water will get wetter, while dry places will get drier. Much drier. Scientists at the National Center for Atmospheric Research predict that by the 2030s, widespread dry conditions will be a reality in the western United States, Latin America (especially Mexico and Brazil), parts of Southwest and Southeast Asia, like China, and most of Africa and Australia. By 2100 these places could experience a level of drought the world has never seen before.

What's wrong with less rain? A lot! It means people have less access to drinking water and can't grow crops or raise livestock, which leads to ***food insecurity*** (lack of access to enough food to eat). African countries including Somalia, Kenya and Ethiopia have faced several years in a row of dry conditions. About 23 million people in the region are hungry. And more than 3 million regularly go at least a day without eating.

In the United States, video-game designer Shayne Hayes and a team at the Atlantic Council's Climate Resilience Center have created a virtual reality (VR) game that gives players a realistic 3D experience of what the future could look like due to climate change. The game is being played by politicians and community leaders so they can see the impact of rising sea levels, floods and storm surges. The gamers can then go back to the present, where they have the ability to make decisions that will change the future. Hayes and his team hope these VR games will help lead to climate action.

PUTTING IDEAS INTO PRACTICE

But there's some hopeful news. In the same way that wet places are learning to become more resilient, dry places can become more resilient too. The United Nations Convention to Combat Desertification and the Food and Agriculture Organization of the United Nations are bringing together scientists, governments and businesses in drought-stricken countries to find ways to ensure that people have water to grow the food they need to survive.

- In India, Brazil and Ethiopia, water from rivers and rainstorms is being collected and saved in tanks so it can be treated and used when needed for drinking and agriculture. The process is called water harvesting.
- In Tanzania, where clean water is scarce and people can't wash their hands properly, hand sanitizer is being given out. Improving hand hygiene prevents diseases and infections.
- In Namibia, farmers are planting different kinds of a grain called millet. Millet is ready for harvesting in a short time (100 days) and grows well even if there isn't a lot of water.

Think about how you can "wash your hands" of water waste at home. Try turning off the tap when you brush your teeth. You can also make sure the washing machine is full before your family does a wash. Same goes for the dishwasher.

Danielle Mayron and her partners are helping save the Dead Sea from shrinking—and from disappearing altogether one day. Although there is conflict between groups in the region, experts from all of them work together on environmental issues that impact their populations. It's called environmental diplomacy.
COURTESY OF DANIELLE MAYRON

IN DEPTH: KEEPING THE DEAD SEA ALIVE

The Dead Sea, a landlocked lake between Israel and Jordan, has been a tourist attraction since ancient times. Its water is so dense with salt that it's impossible to sink. It's 10 times saltier than the average ocean—in fact, it's one of the world's saltiest bodies of water. Known as a sacred site for Jews, Muslims and Christians, the Dead Sea is also famous for its ability to heal everything from asthma to psoriasis. Unfortunately, the Dead Sea is now in crisis. It's shrinking by almost 4 feet (1.2 meters) every year due to climate change and, especially, overexploitation of its natural resources. Since the 1960s the Dead Sea has shrunk by a third, and the decline is expected to continue.

It's sad for Danielle Mayron, an Israeli marine ecologist who is working with Palestinian and Jordanian colleagues to try to save the Dead Sea through an organization called EcoPeace Middle East. "I'm very connected to the Dead Sea," she says.

"As a child we went there with our families and floated in the water. It's the same for Palestinians and Jordanians. It's part of our heritage."

With so much conflict in the region, Mayron says EcoPeace is a perfect opportunity for ***environmental diplomacy***. "We understand that in order to save the Dead Sea and solve our water issues, we have to work together," she says. "If anyone tries to work alone, the environment will suffer. We don't have time to waste."

EcoPeace is working with governments and businesses to get water flowing back into the Dead Sea, in hopes of reversing some of the damage. It is also collaborating on several other projects to ensure that people in the region can water their crops and have clean water to drink. The group educates thousands of visitors each year and speaks at conferences around the world.

The Dead Sea is important to many cultures and has been for centuries. It has special healing properties, which make it a popular attraction for health and leisure. The Dead Sea has so much salt that it's impossible to sink in it.

WESTEND61/GETTY IMAGES

California

THREE
UNDER FIRE

Climate change is responsible for melting glaciers, flooding and drought. It's also created extreme heat and drier conditions in many places around the world—conditions that have caused more wildfires and longer fire seasons than ever before. In fact, annually since 2000 an average of 70,000 wildfires has burned 7 million acres (2.9 million hectares) of forest in the United States. That's more than double the amount of land that went up in flames in the 1990s. Wildfires put people, wildlife and the planet at risk. This chapter will give you a look at some of the places that are burning and need our attention.

Places prone to wildfires, like California, have signs alerting people to that day's potential fire risk. Once a fire gets started, it's hard to put out, and it can have devastating consequences for both humans and wildlife.

STEFANO POLITI MARKOVINA/ SHUTTERSTOCK.COM

DESTINATION: CALIFORNIA

California is famous for sunny days, surfing and celebrities, but it's also becoming known as a wildfire hot spot. In August 2023 wildfires in northern California and Oregon sent plumes of smoke across California. Government agencies told residents to stay indoors and shut their windows.

When smoke from a wildfire gets into people's lungs, it can make them sick. It also reduces air quality, making it hard to breathe, so people should stay indoors.

E4C/GETTY IMAGES

THE INFO EXPRESS

Smoke from wildfires lowers our air quality, making it hard to breathe and unsafe to play outside. Toxins from wildfires may cause thousands of premature deaths in North America each year and put firefighters' lives at risk.

Smoke irritates eyes and throats and can trigger asthma attacks. It's especially dangerous for those who are very young, very old or sick.

Air pollution from wildfires isn't just bad for human health—it's bad for the planet too. Over the last several decades, wildfires in California have become increasingly regular and intense, destroying buildings and burning more land than in previous decades. In fact, California is the most fire-prone state—three times as much land is consumed by fire in California than in any other American state. And California now has 78 more "fire days"—times when conditions are just right for fires to begin—each year than it did 50 years ago. When trees burn, greenhouse gases like carbon dioxide and ***methane*** are released into the air. With

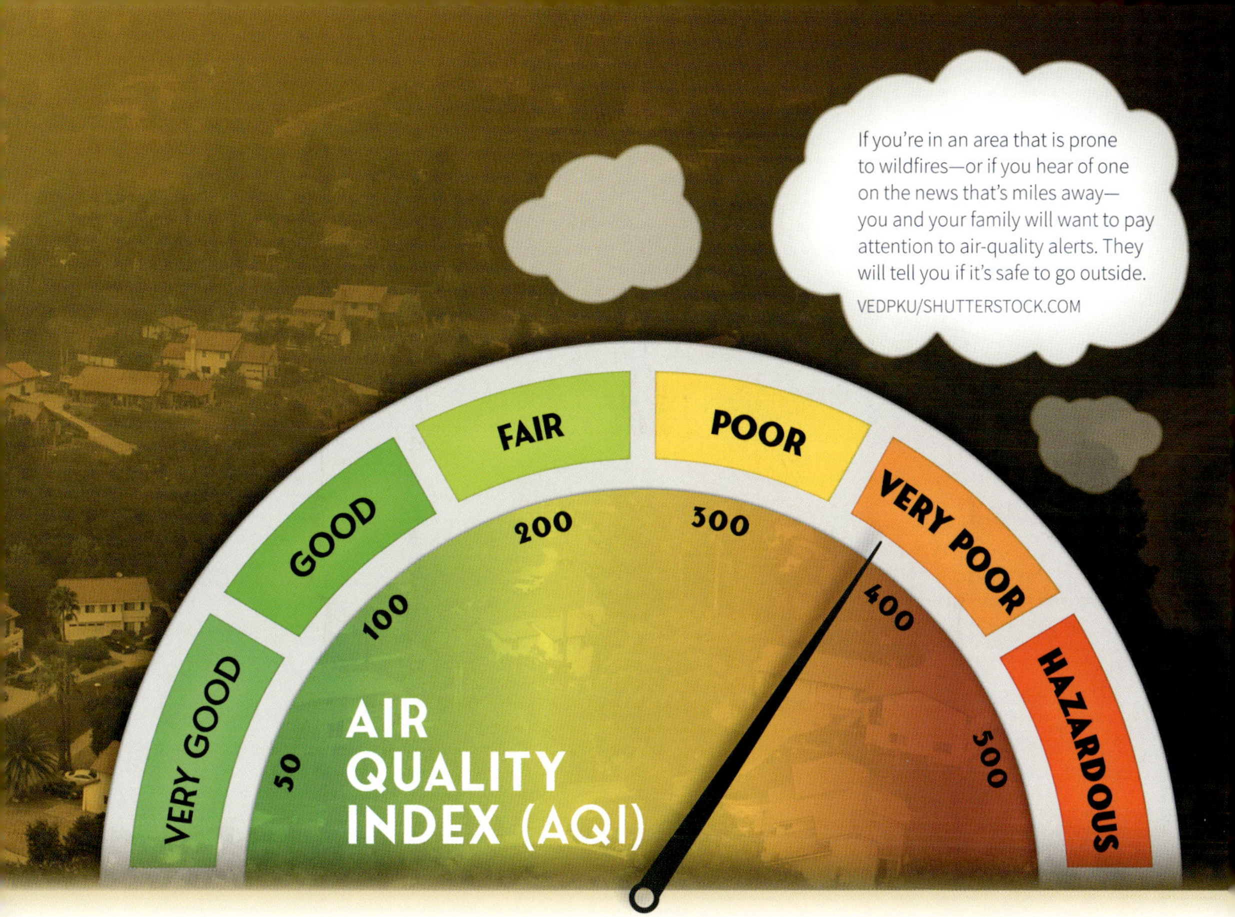

If you're in an area that is prone to wildfires—or if you hear of one on the news that's miles away—you and your family will want to pay attention to air-quality alerts. They will tell you if it's safe to go outside.
VEDPKU/SHUTTERSTOCK.COM

California averaging about 10,000 wildfires per year, out-of-control fires now release about the same amount of carbon as two million cars. Many climate groups are working together to find ways to prevent wildfires from happening in the first place and to manage them more effectively once they start.

FANNING THE FLAMES

Though climate change itself doesn't cause fires, it provides the conditions fires need to burn and spread more easily. The fire behavior triangle shown here illustrates how the combination of weather, fuel (trees, dead branches and dry brush) and topography (features such as slope of the land) impact how fast a fire moves and where it goes.

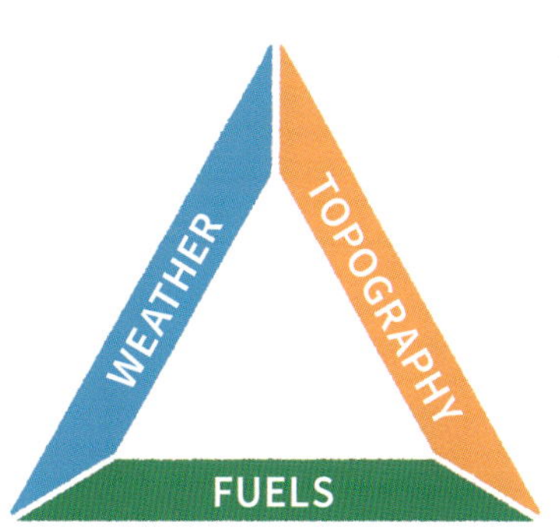

FIGHTING FIRE WITH FIRE

Believe it or not, experts sometimes start fires to fight wildfires. Let me explain! ***Prescribed burns,*** also known as controlled burns, are small fires set on purpose by specially trained experts in order to get rid of excess vegetation that is fuel for fires. Reducing the amount of fuel in the forest means that when there is a wildfire, it's not as big or hard to put out. These fires can also help ***biodiversity***. Getting rid of dead plants makes space for new ones, and the burns may kill off bug-infested trees. Some species of pine and eucalyptus trees need fire to help release their seeds. After a fire, more sunlight reaches the ground. This causes the trees' cones to open and their seeds to spread through the air, leading to new growth and regeneration.

Indigenous communities traditionally and in current times use ***cultural burns*** to keep forests healthy for generations. But since 1850, when the practice was outlawed in California, forests haven't been properly maintained, which has made wildfires worse. Today governments and fire agencies are looking to Indigenous Peoples for expertise on how to use fire properly to make the forest healthy again.

PASSPORT TO MORE: What Causes Wildfires?

Wildfires are unplanned, accidental and uncontrolled fires that typically occur in the summer, when weather is hot, dry and windy. While some statistics show that nearly 90 percent of wildfires are caused by humans—from things like cigarettes, campfires, fireworks and arson—the ones ignited by lightning are usually bigger and burn more land. Climate change causes warmer temperatures, which causes bigger storms and more lightning strikes.

FIRST-RESPONDER THERAPY DOGS: Q&A WITH A FIRE EXPERT

Hawaii is known for its stunning beaches and majestic volcanoes, as well as a climate that produces some of the world's best pineapples, bananas, coffee and nuts.

In recent years this small group of islands has been devastated by wildfires. Fighting fires in the blazing heat for weeks on end is mentally, emotionally and physically exhausting. It can cause firefighters and other first responders like police, paramedics and search-and-rescue teams to feel stressed, depressed or traumatized. Jessica Santa Cruz and her yellow Lab, Cletus, saw this firsthand during Hawaii's devastating wildfires in August 2023. But thanks to the First Responder Therapy Dogs program, first responders in Hawaii and elsewhere are getting some much-needed support.

Q: WHAT IS CLETUS'S JOB AS A FIRST-RESPONDER THERAPY DOG?

A: Dogs are sensitive to emotion. They sense when someone needs support. Cletus will lie there and let firefighters pet him. A lot of people break down and cry because it feels safer to cry to a dog. When I take him to stations or even to the scene of a wildfire, he also boosts morale.

Q: WHAT MAKES FIGHTING FIRES SO STRESSFUL?

A: During fire seasons, first responders may be away from their families for six months in a row. They work 16 hours a day for two to three weeks at a time and camp out in the woods at night. It's stressful and difficult for their mental health, but also their physical health. That's when first-responder dogs come in to help. Thanks to the First Responder Therapy Dogs program, more than 200 therapy dog teams in 37 states have been certified—Cletus is Hawaii's first and only therapy dog in the state.

Q: WHAT DO YOU AND CLETUS DO WHEN IT'S NOT WILDFIRE SEASON?

A: When there isn't a fire in Hawaii, I bring him with me to different communities when I educate people about how to become more fire-wise. I teach people how to protect their homes, how to establish evacuation routes and remind them to check on their neighbors when there is a fire. It's about trying to save lives.

A: Woof, woof!

COURTESY OF JESSICA SANTA CRUZ

You may have been to an overnight camp before, but it's likely nothing like Camp Cinder in California. This free camp for girls ages 16 to 18 teaches participants how to fight forest fires, rescue people from burning buildings and cars and even save people using helicopters. The goal is to get more women involved in the firefighting industry, which needs more helping hands.

Margo Robbins is an Indigenous fire expert in California. The Yurok people are experts at using fires to take care of their land and prevent wildfires from burning out of control. ALLIE HOOTNIK

IN DEPTH: THE IMPORTANCE OF CULTURAL BURNING

Margo Robbins, a member of the Yurok Tribe, is the cofounder and executive director of a nonprofit organization called the Cultural Fire Management Council, located on the Yurok Reservation in northern California. The Yurok people have been maintaining their land with controlled fire for tens of thousands of years. "Our ancestors burned from high up in the mountains down to the ocean to keep the ecosystem in balance and to ensure that the different types of vegetation and animals had a good healthy place to live," says Robbins.

While some areas burn naturally with lightning, the land relies on humans to start fires in other places at certain times of the year. "At one time, our area was 50 percent grassland," says Robbins. "The land was filled with essential food sources like deer, elk, birds and berries, as well as hazel, which is used for weaving baskets."

In the 1800 and 1900s, the state government banned cultural burns and punished Indigenous people with jail or death if they tried to take care of their land with fire. "They didn't understand it," says Robbins. With burns banned, fir trees and invasive plants took over the California coastal prairie, and the ecosystem her ancestors had known disappeared.

Not too long ago, the tide began to change. Governments from California to British Columbia began turning to Indigenous Peoples for expertise in managing fires. "We have put a lot of effort into educating legislators and the public about the need to return fire to its rightful place in the environment," says Robbins. "They are finally recognizing that as [Indigenous People] who have been connected to the land for all these generations and kept it in pristine condition, we know more than a little something about how to take care of the land."

Today cultural burns are allowed at certain times of the year and with safety measures in place. "It's gratifying to see that people appreciate the work that we do fixing the land," says Robbins. The whole family, including young children, participates in cultural burns. "It's critically important for the next generation to learn the how and why of putting fire on our land. It's how we pass on knowledge from generation to generation. My grandkids will never remember a time when we didn't burn. How cool is that?"

British Columbia has had a lot of forests burned by wildfires. These fires have hit the Canadian province hard and caused a lot of damage.

AMIT BASU PHOTOGRAPHY/
GETTY IMAGES

DESTINATION: BRITISH COLUMBIA

Travel to the west coast of Canada and you'll reach the province of British Columbia. Residents love the mild climate, mountain vistas and ocean views. But here, too, wildfires have become a big problem. Although wildfires occur across Canada, British Columbia has the most. In fact, recent wildfire seasons have been some of the most destructive in the province's history.

That's a problem in terms of climate change. Researchers have found that Canada's forests and the soil in which they grow store the equivalent of 40 years of the country's annual greenhouse gas emissions. Trees absorb huge amounts of carbon and keep it out of the atmosphere. But when forests burn, they release more carbon than they store.

BREAKING THE COMBUSTION TRIANGLE

Highly skilled staff with the BC Wildfire Service put out about 1,600 fires each year. They can contain 94 percent of most fires by 10 a.m. the day after they start. Here's how the professionals do it.

OXYGEN
HEAT
FUEL

- **CUT THE HEAT.** The best way for firefighters to cool down a fire is to spray it with water. Crews use a few tools to do this, including water trucks, planes and helicopters.
- **REMOVE FUEL.** Taking out anything that burns, such as grass, trees and bushes, can slow a fire enough for it to burn out on its own. Using equipment like bulldozers or excavators, crews clear wide paths or dirt roads, also called control lines, so there's nothing there to burn.
- **OUST OXYGEN.** Fire retardants, which are basically fertilizer colored bright red, are usually dropped ahead of a fire by special airplanes called air tankers as well as by helicopters. When a fire reaches the retardant, the resulting reaction suffocates the flames. Foam also suppresses a fire by absorbing heat while slowly releasing water at the same time.

Firefighting crews work hard to cool down a fire by spraying it with water.
MOUNTAINBERRYPHOTO/
GETTY IMAGES

Wildlife veterinarians like Jackie Reed take care of animals affected by wildfires and other impacts of climate change.

COURTESY OF JACKIE REED

MEET A WILDLIFE VETERINARIAN

Take a trip down under and you're bound to see a kangaroo or koala. These animals often come to mind when you think of Australia. Jackie Reed has been a wildlife veterinarian in Australia for over 13 years. Of all the animals, koalas are her favorite. "When I treated my first koala, I fell in love with the species, and let's face it, they need all the help they can get," says Reed, who works at Friends of the Koala, a hospital that helps about 350 koalas each year. She is very concerned about the future of this iconic animal. Many of the risks they face are the result of climate change and the bushfires that have ravaged parts of the continent in recent years.

KOALAS AT RISK

"Koalas receive most of their water intake via the leaves they ingest. With increases in temperature, the trees dry out. This causes koalas to become dehydrated and can eventually lead to kidney failure," says Reed. She's talking about the severe drought that led to the bushfire crisis in 2019–20 that killed more than three billion animals in Australia. About 60,000 koalas were either killed, hurt or displaced by the fires.

Wildfires aren't the only climate-related issue koalas face. "We also have floods, which affect koalas as they can drown or may be unable to change trees for an extended period of time," says Reed. "With more frequent climate events, koala numbers will continue to drop." In fact, a combination of factors—including climate change, habitat loss due to human activities, and animal attacks—has caused the koala population to drop so quickly that they're expected to become extinct by 2050.

Reed says, "The animals motivate me to continue doing my absolute best to save each and every one of them that I am lucky enough to treat."

PASSPORT TO MORE: Up in Flames

I recently watched a wildlife documentary called *Breaking Boundaries: The Science of Our Planet.* In it Daniella Teixeira, an ecologist at the University of Queensland in Australia, was moved to tears as she took viewers to a blackened bushfire site. She said the impact of the wildfires was "enormous and consequential." The estimated 3 billion animals that were either killed or displaced include 143 million mammals, 2.46 billion reptiles, 51 million frogs and 180 million birds. With drought and hot temperatures leading to wildfires, scientists worry that Australian summers may never be "normal" again.

PUTTING NATURE AND TECH TO THE TEST

Some new innovations are using nature itself, as well as technology, to help with wildfires. In fact, sometimes they're using a combination of both.

IF TREES COULD TALK

After volunteering to help fight wildfires in Turkey in 2021, a group of university students began to wonder, "What if the trees themselves could notify us that a wildfire has started?" They designed a system of sensors that can detect changes in such things as air temperature, air pressure and gas levels, making it possible to alert firefighters 15 minutes after a wildfire begins. As a comparison, using current technology—thermal images, drones and satellite technology—firefighters learn about fires an average of 90 minutes after they begin. The new system, called ForestGuard, involves strapping fireproof, solar-powered sensors to tree trunks. The team is hoping to expand ForestGuard to countries worldwide.

THE MAGIC OF MUSHROOMS

Concerned about record-high temperatures, drought and an increasing number of wildfires in the United Kingdom, graduate student Suzie McMurtry came up with an idea to detoxify soil after wildfires. She designed a "cannon" that automatically shoots oyster-mushroom spores into a forest after a fire. Why mushroom spores? Fungi have special enzymes, or proteins, that help break down pollutants like pesticides, plastic and oils and turn them into oxygen and carbon. McMurtry's Living with Wildfire system could help regenerate soil after wildfires so new plants can grow again.

FIREFIGHTING ROBOTS

Meet Thermite—the first firefighting super robot in the United States. When it's too hot for firefighters to battle the flames, they send in this 3,500-pound (1,500-kilogram) robotic firefighter. It can shovel debris out of the way and spray water or foam at 2,500 gallons (more than 9,000 liters) a minute. Thermite is equipped with a real-time video feed, so human firefighters can instantly track its efforts in dangerous environments.

Firefighting robots like this one are great helpers. They do a lot of heavy lifting and keep firefighters safe from the flames.

NB/TRAN/ALAMY STOCK PHOTO

New technologies are being developed to help humans track and manage fires once they've broken out. The use of AI helps get important information to fire experts quickly.
KENSTOCKER/GETTY IMAGES

USING AI

Imagine getting a text from a computer about a fire that's broken out. That's exactly what happens when artificial intelligence (AI)—or smart computer systems—analyzes weather satellites. AI gets information to humans quickly, which can mean the difference between being able to put out a fire or it getting out of control. AI can also examine data to help predict a fire's path, crunching numbers and information faster than a human can.

LOOKING UP

When wildfires tear through forests, firefighters rely on drones to gather information, map the path of the fires and help experts plan the best way to get people out of harm's way and put the fires out. Some drones have thermal sensors to show where fires are burning. By capturing video and images in real time, they can help monitor firefighters on the ground to make sure they're safe and recognize when to send in backup. Since they are unmanned and small, drones can get closer to the flames than a helicopter can, keeping pilots safe.

PASSPORT TO MORE: Stop It in Its Tracks

Researchers are experimenting with other kinds of technology to suppress fire. A research lab at Stanford University has developed an environmentally friendly super-absorbent gel that can be sprayed over forests to keep fires in high-risk areas from starting in the first place. This solution is proactive rather than reactive and could end up being a big help to first responders everywhere in the future.

All kinds of cool planes can be used to fight fires from the air.
BRIDGER AEROSPACE/GETTY IMAGES

PASSPORT TO MORE: Taking Flight

From bird dog planes to water skimmers, BC fire crews rely on some much-needed help from the air.

AIR TANKERS: Have tanks filled with fire retardants that are dropped on fires and can hit several targets in one flight.

BIRD DOG PLANES: Fly ahead of air tankers to assess the fire. An air attack officer sits up front and decides where the other aircraft should drop their fire retardant.

JUMPSHIPS: Can take off with a short runway and access hard-to-reach places. They hold parattack crews, also known smoke jumpers, who are trained to parachute out of planes to fight the fire on the ground and help in medical emergencies.

WATER SKIMMERS: Can land on lakes, scoop up water while moving and then drop the water onto the fire.

AMAZON
RAINFOREST

FOUR
LIFE ON EARTH

The world couldn't survive without biodiversity—the variety of animal and plant life in a given environment. From cleaning the air to providing food, homes and even life-saving medicine, our living, breathing world is what sustains our survival. A conservation organization called World Wildlife Fund (WWF) measures the health of biodiversity on Earth through its Living Planet Index. It tracks 32,000 animal species around the world. A 2024 report showed that the population of all species—from mammals and amphibians to fish and birds—has decreased by 73 percent since 1970. Prepare to walk on the wild side as we trek to biodiversity hot spots around the world and learn about some species at risk and what's being done to help them.

There is so much biodiversity in the Amazon, some of the life there hasn't even been discovered yet. School is a great place to start learning about biodiversity and why it's important to protect the Amazon from the impact of climate change.
ANDRESWD/GETTY IMAGES

DESTINATION: THE AMAZON RAINFOREST

Imagine a place so full of life that everywhere you look, you're surrounded by towering trees and the sounds of wildlife.

The Amazon is a rich source of gold, iron, copper and other valuable minerals. In one area of the Amazon, called the Guiana Shield, mining for gold is responsible for 90 percent of ***deforestation***. Trees are being cleared to look for gold and dig mining pits.

Welcome to the Amazon rainforest—the most biologically diverse place on Earth. Unfortunately, the Amazon is so rich with resources that humans use every day that we're destroying it at an alarming rate.

Rainforests around the world are under threat from human activities like cattle ranching, soy farming, palm oil production and unsustainable or illegal logging. But it's an especially big problem in the Amazon rainforest—the world's largest tropical rainforest. It's home to millions of plant and wildlife species, as well as 40 million people, including 1.5 million Indigenous people. This densely packed forested area covers about 40 percent of the landscape in South America, spanning nine countries, including Brazil, Peru, Ecuador and Venezuela. Here's a snapshot of why these forests are disappearing.

Scientists don't know exactly how many species of plants and animals there are on Earth, and estimates range widely, from millions to trillions. Only a fraction of species have been identified and named. Of those species, scientists estimate that many become extinct every day. Sometimes this is a natural process, but the actions of people have sped up the rate of extinction.

THE BEEF WITH RED MEAT

Eighty percent of deforestation in the Amazon results from meeting the world's increasing appetite for beef. The United States and China alone eat almost 33 percent of the world's red meat, but demand for beef is increasing in developing countries too. What does deforestation have to do with beef production? All that land in the Amazon rainforest is being cleared so that cattle have pastures to roam. Even more land is cleared to grow soybeans to feed these animals.

IN THE PALM OF YOUR HAND

The world's demand for palm oil products is another factor that's destroying rainforests. Palm oil is the most popular kind of vegetable oil, and it's found in many products you use every day. Hand soap and shampoo? Check. Candles and cleaning products? Check. Frozen pizza, margarine, cookies and chocolate? Check, check, check and check. We even use it when we fill our cars with gas. Palm oil (and other products that come from it) can be found in about 50 percent of our packaged foods and 70 percent of cosmetics. That's because palm oil makes spreads spreadable, helps food products last longer and ensures that crispy products like potato chips stay crunchy.

LEAST CONCERN

NEAR THREATENED

VULNERABLE

ENDANGERED

CRITICALLY ENDANGERED

EXTINCT IN THE WILD

EXTINCT

Oil palm trees thrive in humid, tropical climates. Because of the demand for palm oil, trees in the Amazon, Indonesia and Africa are being razed and replaced with palm oil plantations. Clearing trees severely impacts and changes the way of life for Indigenous Peoples, for whom the rainforest is home. They rely on the rainforest for shelter, food, medicine and much more. Plantations also destroy the habitat of countless species. Trees absorb carbon, so cutting them down contributes to climate change. Not to mention that when pesticides and fertilizers are used to grow crops like palm oil, soy, rice and sugarcane, the poisons contaminate the water and soil.

FLYING RIVERS DISAPPEAR

Trees are crucial for providing moisture to the Amazon. The rainforest generates huge amounts of water vapor that hang above the treetops. These "flying rivers" provide much-needed moisture, cool the air and keep rainforests hydrated. But climatologists fear we'll reach a point where the rainforest dries up and turns into a desert. They say this tipping

PASSPORT TO MORE: A Barrel of Monkeys

The Amazon rainforest's treetops are home to more than 130 species of monkeys. And some of them are quite remarkable. The pygmy marmoset is the smallest monkey in the world. Howler monkeys are the biggest and loudest—their calls can carry three miles (five kilometers)! Capuchin monkeys use tools like stones to open nuts. And owl monkeys are the world's only monkey species that comes out at night to swing through the trees.

Have you ever visited a rainforest or hiked through a forested area? It's a great way to get fresh air and exercise and learn about all the amazing creatures that rely on the forest for survival.

NOEL HENDRICKSON/GETTY IMAGES

point will come when the Amazon loses 25 percent of its trees. Deforestation has already claimed about 17 percent.

There's some good news, though. A new government in Brazil (home to 60 percent of the Amazon) is doing more to care for the rainforest, such as creating massive areas of protected land. Other countries are beginning to lend a hand. In 2016 Norway became the first country in the world to ban deforestation. Its government won't work with any companies that destroy forests to produce products like soy and beef. In 2008 Norway also gave Brazil $1 billion to save the Amazon rainforest. Within a few years Brazil was able to cut deforestation rates by 75 percent. At a recent United Nations climate summit, more than 100 countries agreed to help stop or reverse deforestation by 2030.

Nat Knowles is fascinated by all she learns by living in the Brazilian rainforest for weeks at a time. During her research, she makes important discoveries and combines what she learns from locals with technology to teach others how to protect this invaluable area.

COURTESY OF NAT KNOWLES

IN DEPTH: TECHNOLOGY, TRADITION AND THE RAINFOREST

For one or two months a year, Nat Knowles calls the Brazilian rainforest her home. She sleeps in a hammock, feasts on delicious fruit and fishes for dinner. It's the adventure of a lifetime for the Canadian conservationist who's on a mission to save the rainforest from deforestation.

"I'm working on a big conservation project with an Indigenous group called the Kayapo. They protect 11 million hectares [27 million acres] of rainforest from deforestation," says Knowles, a researcher at the University of Waterloo in Ontario.

They work with allies, such as Knowles, to ensure that people don't chop down the trees illegally. If the trees disappear, it would be devastating for the local community, the area's rare wildlife species and vast biodiversity, and such elements of the global climate system as rainfall patterns.

"We are right on the edge of where deforestation is happening," says Knowles. "Businesses want the forest for its timber, logging, cattle ranching, soy products and gold mining. These activities are illegal, but there's no law enforcement. The Kayapo people have to protect the entire ecosystem on their own."

Knowles and other conservationists have stepped up to help. For her part, she is working on a special program to help young people ages 15 to 30 learn how to use different kinds of technology, like drones, motion-detection cameras and computers, to conserve their land and protect it.

"We use remote cameras that take pictures of the forest when we're not there. Audio recorders record the songs of birds and frogs so we can see which species are in the forest," Knowles says. "We can take pictures of animals, figure out how many there are and where they are so we can keep them safe."

Her program combines these technologies with Traditional Knowledge from Elders. Knowles says community Elders know more about the forest than most people. "They know what all the plants are, how to use them in herbal medicines and which fruits you can and can't eat."

She says this computer and camera technology is relatively new to the Kayapo people. But by combining tradition with technology, researchers and locals can work together for a common goal. "When I see these places that are worth protecting, whether in images, video or in person, I'm really motivated to help. The world is pretty incredible."

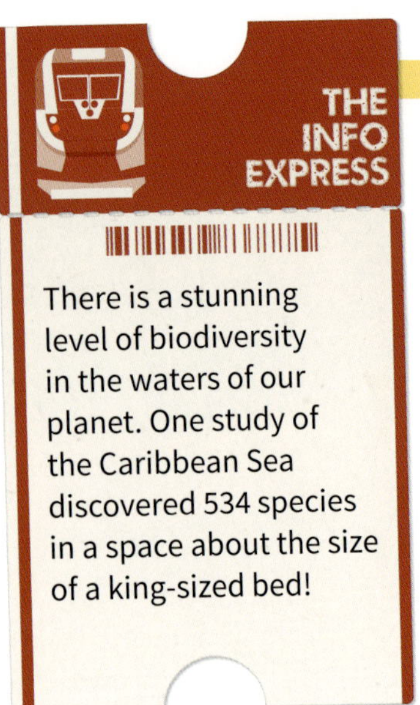

There is a stunning level of biodiversity in the waters of our planet. One study of the Caribbean Sea discovered 534 species in a space about the size of a king-sized bed!

DESTINATION: THE GALÁPAGOS ISLANDS

About 600 miles (965 kilometers) off the coast of Ecuador lie the Galápagos Islands—a series of 19 volcanic islands that have such an abundance of unique plants and animals that the region is known as an ecological treasure. In fact, many of its birds, reptiles, land mammals, marine life and plants can't be found anywhere else in the world. In the last 30 years, climate change has caused the loss of 97 percent of the area's ***coral reefs*** and at least 50 percent of many of its species, including sea lions, iguanas and penguins. Unfortunately, researchers estimate that 150 of these unique species are now endangered or critically endangered, because of climate change, human activity, ***invasive species*** and other challenges.

MANAGING INVASIVE SPECIES

The Galápagos Islands were discovered in 1535. The first permanent settlers arrived in the mid-19th century, bringing with them animals for companionship or food, such as cats and goats and pigs, as well as all kinds of plants the region had never seen before. Visiting ships accidentally brought with them uninvited passengers, including black and brown rats and disease-causing pathogens. Today there are about 1,500 invasive species brought to the islands from other places, and they have had a big impact on native plants and wildlife. The hill raspberry, for example, arrived in the Galápagos from Asia in the 1960s. This plant grows and spreads quickly, forming spiny thickets so dense they prevent native plants from regenerating and birds, such as the colorful vermilion flycatcher, from foraging on the ground for food or having open space in which to eat and breed.

The Galápagos Islands are home to a wide variety of species found nowhere else on this earth.

MANTAPHOTO/GETTY IMAGES

The Galapagos Conservation Trust and several other organizations are working to get rid of nonnative plants like the hill raspberry so that native species can thrive and survive.

MONITORING THE OCEANS

Global warming is one of the biggest threats to biodiversity, with rising temperatures putting many species at risk, especially in the Galápagos. It impacts life on land and in our oceans. Coral reefs—the rainforests of the sea—are one of the most valuable ecosystems on Earth, providing shelter, protection and spawning grounds for a range of marine creatures. The gradual warming of the ocean due to climate change is intensified during El Niño events. The unusually warm surface water places even more stress on corals, causing them to push out the helpful algae in their bodies—which they need to survive—and turn white. This is known as ***coral bleaching***. If the high temperatures persist and the algae don't return, the corals die. And when they die, other plants and animals die. This in turn reduces the food supply for fish, penguins, sea lions, marine iguanas, flightless birds such as the cormorant and other species that live in the Galápagos, and they may starve.

Known as the "father of evolution," Charles Darwin was a British naturalist whose studies in the Galápagos in the 1830s led to groundbreaking theories about how different species grow and thrive. February 12 is the date of his birth and the day the Galápagos Islands became part of Ecuador, so it's a big day. In fact, February 12 is officially Galápagos Day *and* Charles Darwin Day.

BRASTOCK IMAGES/GETTY IMAGES

IT'S (ANOTHER) GIRL!

Climate change poses a different kind of problem for species like turtles, alligators and crocodiles. When they lay eggs, the gender of their babies is based on the temperature of the sand. In warmer sand (above 88°F/31°C), 70 to 90 percent of hatchlings will be female. This leaves a very small number of males. Few species can survive when a population is mainly female. Because increased temperatures mean warmer sand, climate change is putting these creatures' future in jeopardy.

PASSPORT TO MORE: Saving the Great Barrier Reef

The Great Barrier Reef is the largest coral reef system in the world and one of the planet's seven natural wonders. Just imagine it like a colorful underwater mural teeming with sea turtles, fish, coral, sharks and seaweed. Located off the coast of Queensland, Australia, the Great Barrier Reef is so big it can be spotted from outer space. Over the last two decades, warmer ocean temperatures have caused the reefs to cook. Half the reefs have already died, and researchers worry that frequent coral bleaching events will turn the Great Barrier Reef into a graveyard.

PROTECTING BIODIVERSITY IN THE GALÁPAGOS: Q&A WITH A BIOLOGIST

Wacho Tapia Aguilera is a biologist and director of the Galápagos Conservancy, a nonprofit organization dedicated to protecting and restoring the Galápagos Islands. While climate change has caused the loss of much of the area's coral reefs and species, the tide is turning. Thanks to hard work, Tapia Aguilera and his team are seeing some positive changes.

Q: HOW HAVE WARMING TEMPERATURES ON LAND AND IN THE OCEANS IMPACTED BIODIVERSITY IN THE GALÁPAGOS?

A: Climate change has had a profound impact on the Galápagos. The damage has been exacerbated by...excessive rainfall and warmer seas. An overabundance of rain means that invasive species such as blackberry and guava reproduce and spread rapidly, but also provide more food for rats, cats, pigs and other invasive species, which consequently reproduce easily and then prey on our ***endemic*** [native] ***species***. This has led to a reduction in populations of many species, including the giant tortoises, of which we now only have 10 percent of the population that existed before human presence in the Galápagos.

Q: WHAT ARE EXAMPLES OF WORK YOU'RE DOING TO PROTECT LAND SPECIES FROM INVASIVE SPECIES?

A: On Pinzón Island, the Galápagos National Park managed to eradicate introduced rats, allowing giant tortoises born on the island to survive without human assistance...On Isabela Island, we supported cat and rat control and other conservation actions to ensure the survival of the pink iguana. We are also releasing giant tortoises back into the wild to contribute to the restoration of their ecosystems.

Q: WHAT CAN BE DONE TO BRING BACK THE CORAL REEFS?

A: Since 2022 we have supported the national park in developing a technique for successfully reproducing small corals to restore the reefs. The reproduced corals are kept in a nursery and will eventually be released into the ocean on a larger scale.

Q: WHY IS IT SO IMPORTANT TO PROTECT THE GALÁPAGOS?

A: People around the world think that humans are the main species and can do whatever we want. This is a significant error because we are part of the ecosystem and need to understand that we depend on nature for our existence. The Galápagos is a place where most of the ecosystems and biodiversity are protected and are part of humanity's natural heritage. We can become an example of the possibility of finding harmony between humans and nature.

Q: DO YOU THINK THERE WILL BE A TIME WHEN WILDLIFE ON THE GALÁPAGOS WILL HAVE RECOVERED?

A: Yes, absolutely. We are on the right path, but we need to continue our work, and we need people to understand the importance of protecting biodiversity.

Wacho Tapia Aguilera and his team at the Galápagos Conservancy work together to protect vulnerable species and make sure they survive amid the challenges they face because of climate change.

COURTESY OF THE GALÁPAGOS CONSERVANCY

SUSTAINABILITY CHAMPIONS ACROSS THE GLOBE

In many countries, young people just like you are making a difference and protecting biodiversity.

- Mya-Rose Craig, an environmentalist and bird lover from the United Kingdom, created an initiative called Black2Nature to inspire young people from diverse backgrounds to get involved in conservation. They host nature walks, tree-planting events and camps to connect young people with nature.

- Talk about teamwork! After seeing the negative impact of plastic bags on their island of Bali, two sisters, Melati and Isabel Wijsen, founded the Bye Bye Plastic Bags campaign to get rid of plastic bags. Their work eventually led the Balinese government to ban plastic bags on the island.

- A group of young people in India made headlines when they cleaned up beaches where sea turtles come to lay their eggs. This gave the turtles a safe place to lay and hatch their eggs, increasing the number of hatchlings.

It's so important for young people to get involved in helping the planet. There are many organizations and groups that need help with protecting the environment!

ERIK GINANJAR NUGRAHA

MEET A CLIMATE ADVENTURER

Ray Zahab is a Canadian adventurer, ultra (long-distance) runner and founder of impossible2Possible. It's a nonprofit organization that takes groups of youth ambassadors on grueling trips around the world and live streams their adventures to classrooms everywhere through satellite technology. Zahab has experienced every extreme you can imagine, from the hottest summer on Earth in Death Valley, California, to one of the most remote places, Kamchatka Peninsula in far eastern Russia. He's seen the effects of climate change firsthand.

I managed to talk to Zahab between expeditions.

"I had a hard time in school," he says from his home in Quebec. "I was disinterested in learning from textbooks, but when I was on adventures, I wanted to learn about everything around me. That connection between adventure and learning is why I started impossible2Possible. I'm not a scientist, but as an adventurer, I learn from people who live in places wherever I go."

A PUNCH IN THE FACE

Zahab started the nonprofit with his friend Bob Cox in 2008. "If you're going to talk about climate change and biodiversity, you really need to speak to people who live [in affected places] to learn about the issues they face and how they're adapting to their environment."

Schoolkids were transfixed when Zahab and a group of youth ambassadors, who ranged in age from 17 to 21, ran across Botswana in Africa. During the expedition, students were able to watch the adventure unfold via live stream. They saw the impact of drought on the country and learned about the importance of water.

Ray Zahab has explored areas of extremes, from the scorching heat of deserts to the frigid cold of Russia. He live streams his adventures to give students a firsthand look at the world we live in.
JON GOLDEN

Live-stream viewers also got to learn about climate change during Zahab's visits to Death Valley. He traveled there during back-to-back years of record-setting temperatures. "It was so hot it was like reaching into a pizza oven. I had the sensation like my fingernails were burning."

He said the experience felt like "a punch in the face"—he found it upsetting that "a good part of the world is becoming like a furnace. This heat isn't survivable, and that's a scary thought."

Zahab's goal, however, isn't to scare people. "My goal is to give kids a chance to pop into places, to learn, to share what they're learning and become leaders and decision-makers," he says. "I want to inspire an entire generation of youth to want to learn more and preserve our planet."

HARNESSING YOUR POWER

Researching this book was overwhelming. At least, at first. How am I as a writer, or you as a reader, supposed to save so many places from being destroyed? Climate change seems just too big a problem for us to stop. I diagnosed myself with a case of climate anxiety—that's extreme worry about the future of the planet.

But as I kept going in my research, I met architects, wildlife experts, artists, skaters and scientists all working in their own unique ways to make a difference in at-risk places across the world. I was especially happy when I realized that books like this, and readers like you, are also a huge part of the solution. That's because kids have a lot more power than they might think.

Earth Rangers is just one of many eco clubs you can join to learn more about climate change. Maybe your school has one. Why not get involved?
WESTEND61/GETTY IMAGES

TAKE ACTION

According to Stephanie Doyle, a climate educator at a charity called Earth Rangers, it's all thanks to a phenomenon called the pass-through effect. "Kids get through to adults more easily than the government," says Doyle, whose organization offers clubs and programs for kids, researches eco-anxiety and produces podcasts about climate change. (I listened to their podcast when I was writing this book!)

"If a child comes home from school after having learned about the impact of single-use plastics on the planet and tells their parents they should all be drinking tap water, parents will most likely do it," says Doyle.

Even 10-year-olds like my friend Nate, whom I mentioned at the start of this book, can make an impact. "A 10-year-old can't vote. But we encourage [club] members to contact people who can vote," Doyle says. "Write a letter to an elected official to say what needs to change. It's different when kids talk to adults than when adults talk to adults. Kids have power they can harness."

Doyle tells schoolkids that it's okay to be afraid about climate change and encourages them to talk about it. It's also important that they educate themselves about the issues, so they're informed and inspired to take care of the planet. When we feel empowered to take action, we can be excited about the impact we've made.

I couldn't wait to share what I'd learned with Nate. If we all do our part, he may one day float in the Dead Sea. In fact, he might even be one of the people who helps save it. It's possible you will be too.

YOU CAN MAKE POSITIVE CHANGES TODAY!

In the documentary *Breaking Boundaries: The Science of Our Planet,* the famous biologist David Attenborough says that what we do now is decisive for our future. By acting now, we can help life on Earth and improve all our lives. Here are a few small, simple changes we can make to help ourselves and biodiversity.

- Think about the products you buy. I was excited when I noticed the Sustainable Forestry Initiative logo on my milk carton. The logo means that my milk container was made of recycled material or material from certified forests. *Certified* in this context means that conservation was a top priority and that trees were harvested in a way that protects forests, water quality, biodiversity and wildlife habitat. You can look for products with the Forest Stewardship Council or Rainforest Alliance Certified logos.

- Plant a garden in your backyard or hang a bird feeder so wildlife like bees and birds have a healthy habitat in which to pollinate, eat and live. When you go to parks, look at the flowers—don't trample them. And don't rip leaves off trees.

- Consider your eating habits. Cut back on how much red meat you eat or ask the adults in your life to buy meat raised on sustainable farms—both will help reduce deforestation. Have more fruits, vegetables and nuts, and avoid products made with palm oil—that's another way to reduce your carbon footprint. It takes valuable resources to grow food, so try not to waste it.

- Plant trees to absorb more carbon and combat climate change. Maybe you can get your hands dirty by participating in a local tree-planting day in your community. Check out One Tree Planted (onetreeplanted.org), a nonprofit organization dedicated to planting trees all over the world, to learn how you can get involved no matter where you live.

- Cut down on paper. Can you do more things electronically or talk to your teacher about using double-sided handouts at school? Whenever you can, make sure the paper you use has already been recycled—and then recycle it when you're done.

- Educate others. Share what you've learned with friends, family and classmates. Talk to your teachers about ways your school can be more sustainable.

Getting out in nature is a great way to appreciate the value of the world we live in—it might even inspire you to help protect it.
ASCENTXMEDIA/GETTY IMAGES

ARTMARIE/GETTY IMAGES

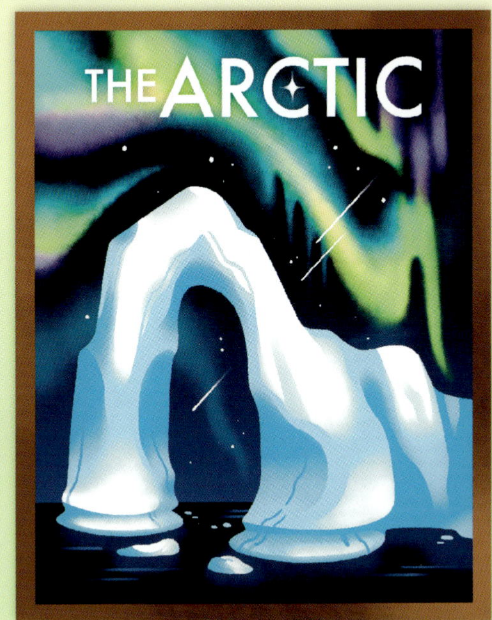
THE ARCTIC

PACIFIC ISLANDS

Calif
AMAZON
RAINFOREST

GLOSSARY

biodiversity—the variety of plant and animal life in a given environment

carbon dioxide—a greenhouse gas that traps heat in the atmosphere and contributes to global warming

carbon footprint—the amount of carbon dioxide released into the air by the activities of a person, company or country; in other words, the impact we have on the planet

carnivore—an animal that eats only animal products, mostly meat

climate change—long-term shifts in temperatures and weather patterns. Since the 1800s, humans have been the main cause of these shifts.

climate migrants—people who have to leave their homes and communities because of the effects of climate change

climate resilience—the ability to prepare for, adapt to or recover from the impacts of climate change

coral bleaching—the result of unusually warm seawater, which causes corals to push out the algae living in them and turn white. The corals will eventually die if the ocean doesn't cool.

coral reefs—diverse underwater ecosystems found in tropical areas all over the world that help support life in the ocean

cultural burns—controlled, low-intensity fires set in specific areas by Indigenous people at low-risk times of year to protect their land and way of life

dams/dikes/floodgates/levees—barriers built across water bodies to prevent land from flooding during storm surges or when water levels rise too high

dead zones—areas with oxygen levels so low that little can survive there. Some form naturally, but most are the result of pollution from agriculture or the effects of climate change.

decarbonize—to reduce or remove carbon

deforestation—the clearing of forests by humans so the land can be used as farmland for livestock or crops or the trees can be used for lumber

ecosystems—all the living and nonliving things in an area, working together as a system

El Niño—a pattern of unusual warming of the surface waters in the eastern tropical Pacific Ocean. The warm current can cause catastrophic weather conditions. La Niña usually follows, bringing cool ocean currents and the opposite kind of extreme weather.

endangered—threatened with extinction

endemic species—species found only in a particular place or habitat

environmental diplomacy—an effort by governments and international institutions to address environmental problems that affect them all

Equatorial Pacific Ocean—a region of the Pacific Ocean near the equator

food insecurity—the state of having inadequate or uncertain access to nutritious food

food security—the state of having reliable access to nutritious food

glaciers—large bodies of ice formed over time by compacted layers of snow

geoengineering—artificial alteration of the environment to manage or lessen the effects of climate change

glaciologist—a scientist who studies snow, ice and glaciers

global warming—the long-term rise in Earth's average temperature, caused by human activity

greenhouse gases—gases that traps heat near Earth's surface, warming the planet and contributing to the climate crisis. They include carbon dioxide, methane and nitrous oxide.

ice caps—large masses of ice and snow that cover areas that are less than 19,000 square miles (50,000 square kilometers). They submerge the land beneath them.

ice sheets—thick sheets of ice that cover areas that are more than 19,000 square miles (50,000 square kilometers). Mountains and ridges may protrude from them.

invasive species—nonnative plants, animals or other living things that are introduced to a new habitat and change or harm that environment

land subsidence—gradual or sudden sinking of Earth's surface

meltwater—water from melting ice and snow, which feeds lakes, rivers and streams

methane—a greenhouse gas that contributes to global warming. Its largest sources are agriculture (cattle release a lot of methane gas), the fossil-fuel industry and decomposition of landfill waste.

microplastics—tiny pieces of plastic that don't break down and are harmful to animals and humans

oxygen—a colorless gas that makes up a large part of the air we breathe and is essential for life

photosynthesis—the process of converting sunlight, carbon dioxide and water into oxygen and energy

prescribed burns—fires that are planned and managed by experts, in order to keep an ecosystem healthy

storm surges—rises in water level, generated by storms, that are above normal tidal levels

synthetic—produced artificially

water towers—a tower with a water tank, whose height creates the pressure required to distribute the water through a piped system

RESOURCES

PRINT

BOOKS:

Arbuthnott, Gill. *From Shore to Ocean Floor: The Human Journey to the Deep.* Big Picture Press, 2023.

Barr, Catherine, and Steve Williams. *The Story of Climate Change: A First Book About How We Can Help Save Our Planet.* Frances Lincoln Children's Books, 2021.

Clinton, Chelsea. *Don't Let Them Disappear: 12 Endangered Species Across the Globe.* Philomel Books, 2019.

DK. *Eyewitness: The Amazon.* DK Children, 2022.

Herman, Gail. *What Is Climate Change?* Penguin Workshop, 2018.

Kirby, Loll. *Old Enough to Save the Planet.* Harry N. Abrams, 2021.

Minoglio, Andrea. *Our World Out of Balance: Understanding Climate Change and What We Can Do.* Blue Dot Kids Press, 2021.

Pettiford, Rebecca. *Coral Reef Food Chains.* (Who Eats What? series.) Pogo Books, 2017.

Roth, Annie. *Amazing Oceans: The Surprising World of Our Incredible Seas.* DK Children, 2023.

Sanchez, Anita. *Meltdown: Discover Earth's Irreplaceable Glaciers and Learn What You Can Do to Save Them.* Workman Publishing Company, 2022.

Scales, Helen. *Scientists in the Wild: Galápagos.* Flying Eye Books, 2023.

MAGAZINES:

Eco Kids Planet: ecokidsplanet.co.uk

National Geographic Kids: kids.nationalgeographic.com/magazine

OWL Magazine: owlkids.com

The Week Junior: kids.theweekjunior.com

RESOURCES

ONLINE

DOCUMENTARIES:

A Beautiful Planet. Directed by Toni Myers. IMAX and Walt Disney Studios, 2016.

Breaking Boundaries: The Science of Our Planet. Directed by Jonathan Clay. Indikate Productions and Silverback Films, 2021.

Chasing Coral. Directed by Jeff Orlowski. Exposure Labs, 2017.

To the Arctic. Directed by Greg MacGillivray. MacGillivray Freeman Films, 2012.

PODCASTS:

Earth Rangers

Nature Breaking

The Big Melt

WEBSITES:

CLEAN: Committed to Climate Change and Energy Education: cleanet.org

Climate Action Families: climateactionfamilies.org

Earth Science Week: earthsciweek.org

Jane Goodall's Roots & Shoots United States: rootsandshoots.org

Jet Propulsion Laboratory: jpl.nasa.gov

Just for Kids Climate Change Resources: climatechangeresources.org/youth/just-for-kids/

NASA Climate Kids: climatekids.nasa.gov

National Geographic Kids: kids.nationalgeographic.com

NPR: A Kid's Guide to Climate Change: npr.org/2023/01/17/1144849154/climate-change-kids-guide

Polar Bears International: polarbearsinternational.org

Sustainability for All: activesustainability.com

Toronto Zoo: torontozoo.com

World Wildlife Fund Wild Classroom: worldwildlife.org/teaching-resources

Youth Climate Lab: youthclimatelab.org

ACKNOWLEDGMENTS

It takes a village to bring a book to life, and I have so many people to thank for this one. First of all, to Nate and Danya, for sharing this amazing idea with me. You are both such a source of inspiration—thank you for thinking of me! As I began my research, several people and organizations stepped up to help. Thank you to:

- Amy Naylor and Erica Jacques at the Toronto Zoo for teaching me about polar bears.
- Dr. Alison Criscitiello for telling me all about her ice-core research and sharing her love of the planet with budding explorers. She also helped review the chapter on melting glaciers and ice caps.
- Colin Parker for chatting with me about his passion for extreme adventure art.
- Elladj Baldé for taking some time off the ice to talk to me about his passion for winter sports.
- Mary Liesegang, program coordinator at Antarctic and Southern Ocean Coalition, for talking to me about what it's like to explore the Antarctic.

Chapter 2 could not have come together without Amy Chester, managing director of Rebuild by Design; Deni Purwandana, chairman of the Komodo Survival Program in Indonesia; climate architect Flemming Rafn in Denmark; Shayne Hayes, a video-game designer dedicated to putting a dent in climate change; and, especially, Danielle Mayron, an Israeli marine ecologist who is working with Palestinian and Jordanian colleagues to try to save the Dead Sea through an organization called EcoPeace Middle East. She spoke to me at length during a war about her close relationship with her colleagues, and it left us both in tears. Another special thank-you goes to Professor Elizabeth English, founder of the Buoyant Foundation Project and professor at the University of Waterloo in Ontario. Thanks for reviewing the chapter about flooding.

Thank you to burn boss Margo Robbins for talking to me about cultural burning in California; Dr. Jackie Reed for sharing her passion for saving koalas in Australia; Jessica Santa Cruz for teaching me about her work as a firefighter and educator in Hawaii; and Dr. Jennifer Baltzer, Canada Research Chair in Forests and Global Change and professor in the Department of Biology, Wilfrid Laurier University, for reviewing the wildfire chapter.

And, finally, chapter 4 would not have been possible without the expertise of the amazing Canadian conservationist Nat Knowles for telling me about her experience in Brazil and all the other research she's done about warming winters; Xavier Castro and Wacho Tapia Aguilera from the Galápagos Conservancy; and Ray Zahab, the amazing cofounder of impossible2Possible.

Of course, my wonderful team at Orca, including Kirstie Hudson, Maria Birmingham, Georgia Bradburne and Kaedra Becker, deserve a big shout-out. I'm so grateful for the opportunity to work on another book with you. Here's to many more!

INDEX

activism
consumer choice, 16, 57–58, 72–73
to raise awareness, 13, 18–19, 35–37
tree planting, 73
of youth, 16, 66–67, 70–73
agriculture
drought, 14, 34–35
impact on rainforests, 56–58
Alaska, oil spill, 12
Amazon rainforest
preservation, 58–61
pressures on, 55–58
Antarctic, 5–9
Arctic
endangered landscapes, 19
research, 14–15, 20–21
risks to, 10–13
art as activism, 19
Attenborough, David, 72
Australia
Great Barrier Reef, 64
severe storms, 25
wildfires, 48–49

Baldé, Elladj, 18
Bangkok, Thailand, 27, 30
beef production, 57
biodiversity
conservation, 60–61
and controlled burns, 42
defined, 55, 76
extinction rate, 55, 57
and invasive species, 62–63
blue whale, 9
Brazil, rainforest, 59–61
British Columbia, wildfires, 46–47

California, wildfires, 39–45
Canada, wildfires, 44
carbon dioxide
capture, 8, 9, 46, 58
emissions, 40–41, 76
carbon footprint, 18, 76
Chester, Amy, 29
China, 57
cities
flooding of, 23, 25, 27–33
and land subsidence, 26, 28, 78
climate change
and agriculture, 14, 34–35, 56–58
carbon footprint, 18, 76
defined, 76
and forests, 39, 41, 42, 46
and human migration, 26, 27
rate of, 1, 2, 7, 11
role of governments, 37, 59, 71
stabilizing of, 8, 11
See also global warming
climate migrants, 26, 27, 76
climate resilience, 29, 35, 76
clothing, synthetic, 21
coastlines, 12, 24, 28, 67
conservation. *See* environmental research
consumer choice, 16, 57–58, 72–73
coral reefs, 62–64, 65, 76
Cox, Bob, 68
Craig, Mya-Rose, 66
Criscitiello, Alison, 14–16
cultural burns, 42, 76

dams/dikes/floodgates/levees, 28, 30, 76
Darwin, Charles, 63
Dead Sea, 36–37
dead zones, 21, 76
Death Valley, CA, 69
deforestation, 46, 56–58, 76
Denmark, 31
Doyle, Stephanie, 70–71
drought, 34–37, 49

ecosystems
Antarctic, 5–9
coral reefs, 62–64, 65, 76
defined, 77
forest, 42, 44–45
and invasive species, 62–63
and oil spills, 12
rainforests, 55–61
El Niño, 25, 46, 63, 77
endangered species, 13, 26, 49, 55, 57–58, 77
endemic species, 65, 77
English, Elizabeth, 32
environmental diplomacy, 37, 77
environmental research, 6, 14–16, 20–21, 51, 60–61
See also geoengineering
Equatorial Pacific Ocean, 25, 77

flooding
amphibious houses, 32
causes, 8, 23, 25
control of, 27–33
floating parking lots, 31, 32
land subsidence, 26, 28, 78
low-lying islands, 24
and mangrove forests, 28
severe storms, 23, 25
use of parkland, 29, 30
and wildlife, 26
food insecurity/security, 11, 14, 34, 77
forests
deforestation, 46, 56–58, 76
forestry, 42, 44–45, 50–51
mangrove, 28
fresh water
habitat, 11
pollution, 15
supply, 6, 14, 15, 34–35

Galápagos Islands, 62–67
geoengineering
defined, 77
flooding control, 27–33
reducing glacier melt rate, 20–21
Girls on Ice Canada, 15
glaciers
Antarctic, 5–9
Arctic, 11
defined, 77
ice caps/ice sheets, 5–9, 11, 77
mountain, 14–15
reducing melt rate, 20–21
research, 14–16
and sea level rise, 1, 8, 23
global warming
and biodiversity, 63, 65
defined, 77
and deforestation, 46, 56–58, 76
effects of, 18, 23
and glaciers, 5–8
and ocean currents, 8, 25, 46, 63
rate of, 1, 2, 7
and sea ice, 11

governments, role of, 37, 59, 71
Great Barrier Reef, 64
greenhouse gases
  defined, 77
  emissions, 1, 40–41, 46

Hawaii, wildfires, 43
Hayes, Shayne, 35
Himalayan glaciers, 14
housing, floating, 32
Hurricane Katrina, 30

ice caps/ice sheets, 5–9, 11, 77
  See also glaciers
Indigenous Peoples
  Arctic, 10, 11–12
  cultural burns, 42, 44–45
  and rainforest preservation, 56, 60–61
invasive species, 62–63, 65, 78
islands, low-lying, 24

Jacques, Erica, 12–13
Jakarta, Indonesia, 26

Knowles, Nat, 60–61
koala, 48–49
Komodo dragon, 26
krill, 9

land subsidence, 26, 28, 78

mangrove forests, 28
Mayron, Danielle, 36–37
McMurtry, Suzie, 51
meltwater, 14, 78
methane, 40, 78
Miami, FL, 27
microplastics, 15, 16, 21, 78
mining, 12, 56
monkeys, 58

nature, experience of, 19, 66, 68–69
New Orleans, LA, 29
New York City, NY, 27, 29
Norway, 59

oceans
  biodiversity of, 62
  covering land, 24
  currents, 8, 25, 46, 63
  dead zones, 21, 76
  El Niño, 25, 46, 63, 77
  salmon fishery, 11–12
  sea level rise, 8, 23
  warming, 63, 64
oil drilling, 12
Olympics, winter, 17–18
oxygen
  defined, 78
  and fires, 47
  and plant life, 9, 51

Pacific Islands, 24
Pacific Ocean
  El Niño, 25, 46, 63, 77
  Equatorial, 25, 77
palm oil production, 57–58
Parker, Colin, 19
penguins, 5, 9, 11
permafrost, 8
photosynthesis, 9, 78
phytoplankton, 9
plastic bag, banning, 67
polar bears, 12–13
pollution
  in the Arctic, 12
  dead zones, 21, 76
  microplastics, 15, 16, 21, 78
  wildfires, 39–41
prescribed burns, 42, 78

Rafn, Flemming, 31
rainforests
  preservation, 58–61
  pressures on, 55–58
Reed, Jackie, 48–49
resources, 79–80
Robbins, Margo, 44–45

sacred sites, 36–37
salmon fishery, 11–12
Santa Cruz, Jessica, 43
schools
  activism, 16, 70–71
  projects, 32–33
sea ice, 11, 13
sea turtles, 64, 67
Shanghai, China, 27
Singapore, 30
species
  endangered, 13
  endemic, 65, 77
  invasive, 62–63, 65, 78
sports, winter, 16–18, 20
storm surges, 25, 78
stormwater, 25, 27, 30, 33

Tapia Aguilera, Wacho, 65, 66
technology
  and firefighting, 50–53
  flooding control, 27–33
  for rainforest preservation, 60–61
  reducing glacier melt rate, 20–21
  virtual reality VR, 35
Teixeira, Daniella, 49
Tokyo, Japan, 27
tortoises, giant, 65
tourism
  Antarctic, 7
  Dead Sea, 36–37
  future opportunities, 1–2
Tropical Cyclone Jasper, 25
turtles, alligators and crocodiles, 64, 67

United Nations, 35, 59
United States
  beef consumption, 57
  wildfires, 39

Venice, Italy, 28

water
  pollution, 15, 21
  river habitat, 11
  supply, 6, 14, 15, 34–35
weather, extreme, 1, 8, 23, 25, 27–33
Wijsen, Melati and Isabel, 67
wildfires
  air quality alerts, 39–41
  causes, 42
  firefighters, 43–44, 47
  fire suppression, 47, 50–53
  impact on wildlife, 48–49
  prevention, 42, 44–45, 52
wildlife
  and dead zones, 21, 76
  endangered, 13, 26, 49, 55, 57–58, 77
  extinction rate, 55, 57
  habitat loss, 49, 58
  impact of climate change, 9, 11–13, 48–49, 63–65
winter sports, 16–18, 20

youth
  activism, 16, 66–67, 70–73
  as ambassadors, 68–69
  programs for girls, 15, 44

Zahab, Ray, 68–69

MORE NONFICTION BY AWARD-WINNING AUTHOR ERIN SILVER

Trendy clothes, electronics, fast food and plastic gift cards. These days, there's plenty to buy, but we're purchasing things and throwing them out at an alarming rate. And our shopping habits are hurting the planet. By changing what you buy and how often, small decisions can make a big difference!

"THIS AN APPEALING AND INFORMATIVE BOOK FOR YOUNG PEOPLE LOOKING FOR WAYS TO FIGHT CLIMATE CHANGE BY HELPING US EVOLVE FROM A DISPOSABLE TO REUSABLE SOCIETY." –*BOOKLIST*

Sports have a big impact on the environment, and athletes are also feeling the effects of global warming. From skiing to baseball, sports and the climate crisis are facing off. But organizations, athletes and fans are taking action to change the rules of the game.

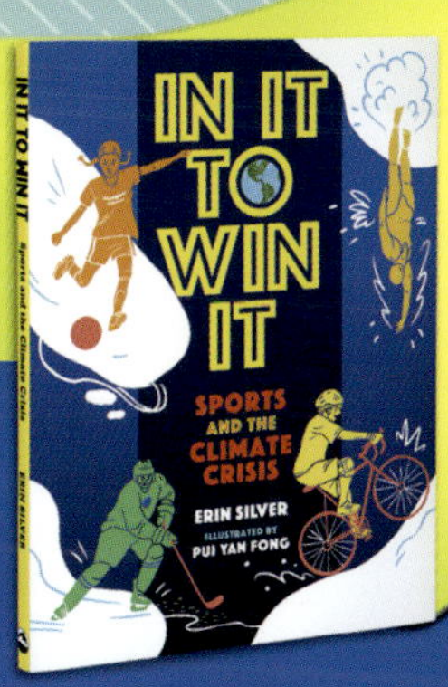

"SILVER'S TONE IS UPBEAT THROUGHOUT, URGING YOUNG ATHLETES TO BE PART OF THE 'WINNING TEAM' BY MAKING SMALL BUT IMPACTFUL CHANGES." –*SCHOOL LIBRARY JOURNAL*

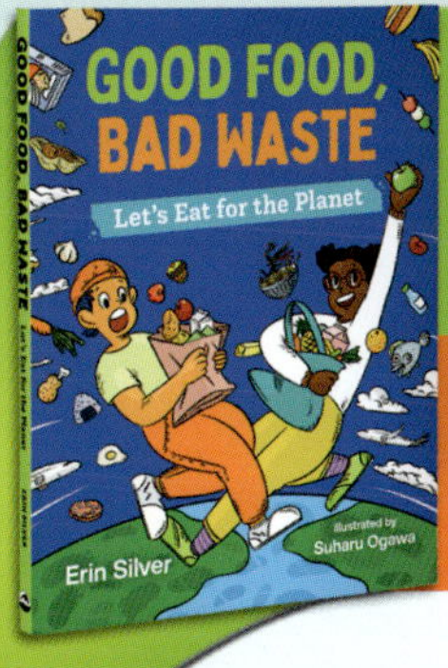

Every day good food gets tossed in the trash. Around the world, a billion tons of food gets thrown away every year. Discover why we waste so much and the consequences for people and the planet. Kids can help fight the problem starting at home!

"A THOROUGH, UPBEAT LOOK AT THE PROBLEM OF FOOD WASTE." –*KIRKUS REVIEWS*

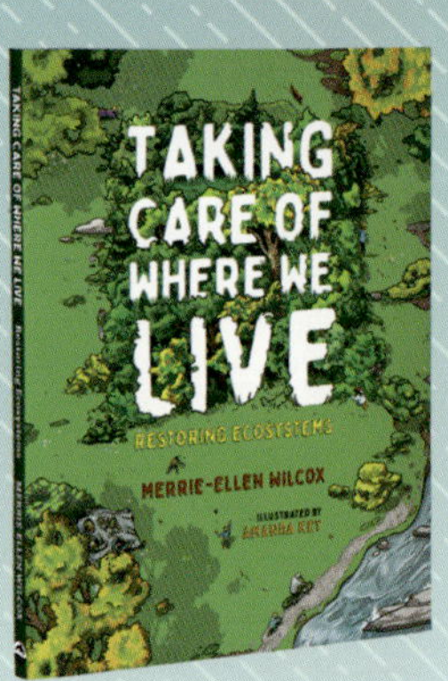

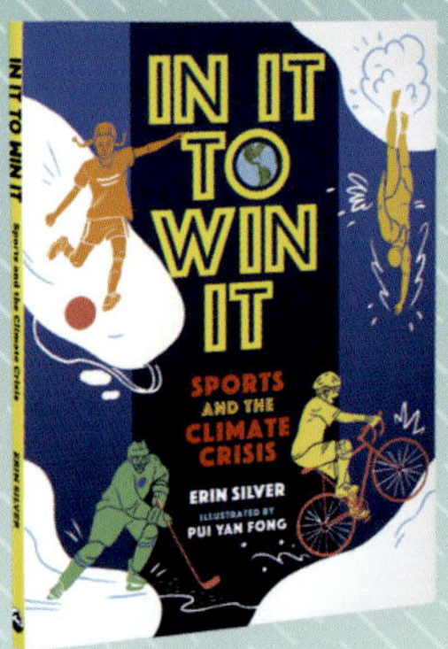

ALONE TOGETHER
A CURIOUS EXPLORATION OF LONELINESS
PETTI FONG
ILLUSTRATED BY JONATHAN DICK

REMEMBER THIS
The Fascinating World of Memory
Monique Polak
Illustrated by Valéry Goulet

THE MORE YOU GROW

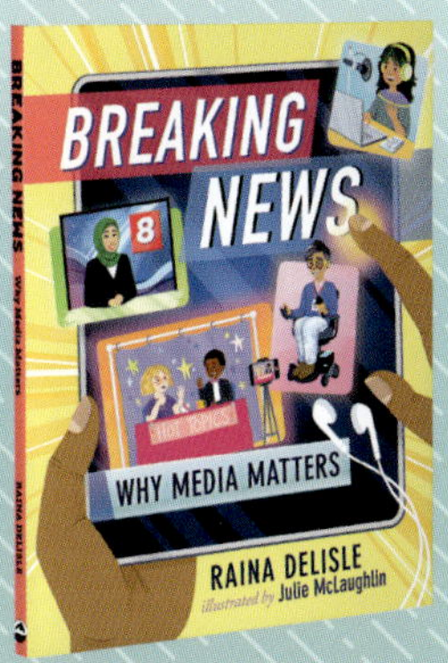

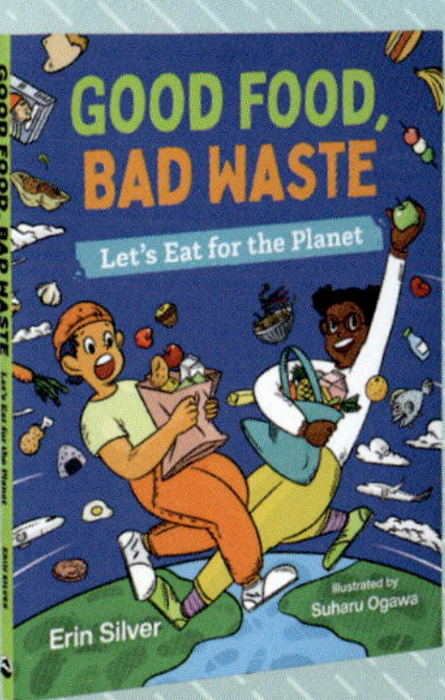

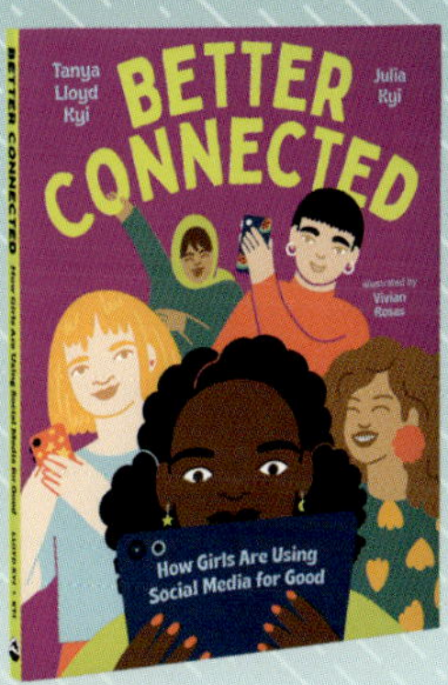

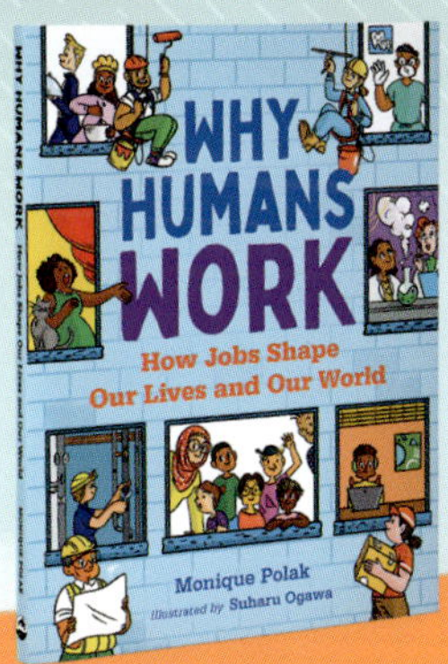

The **Orca Think** series introduces us to the issues making headlines in the world today. It encourages us to question, connect and take action for a better future. With those tools we can all become better citizens. Now that's smart thinking!

MAGENTA PHOTO STUDIO

Erin Silver is an award-winning children's author and freelance writer. Her books for children include *Just Watch Me* (Crystal Kite Award nominee), *What Kids Did: Stories of Kindness and Invention in the Time of COVID-19* (Hackmatack Award nominee), *Proud to Play: Canadian LGBTQ+ Athletes Who Made History*, *Rush Hour: Navigating Our Global Traffic Jam* (Blueberry Award winner), *Sitting Shiva* (Ontario Library Association Best Bets, Sydney Taylor Book Award Honor, Vine Award finalist, TD Canadian Children's Literature Award finalist), *Good Food, Bad Waste: Let's Eat for the Planet*, *Mighty Scared: The Amazing Ways Animals Defend Themselves*, *In It to Win It: Sports and the Climate Crisis* and *All Consuming: Shop Smarter for the Planet.*

ANDREW LOVE

Xulin Wang is an award-winning Canadian Chinese illustrator, cartoonist, writer and muralist based in Toronto. They write and illustrate comics at the intersection of science and social justice. As a lifelong learner passionate about education and science communication, they've dedicated their career to translating complex ideas into compelling and understandable illustrations. They are the illustrator of *Can We Talk?: How Humans Stay in Touch*, part of the Orca Timeline series.

BRITISH
COLUMBIA

GREAT BARRIER
REEF

GALÁPAGOS

CALIFORNIA

Hawaii

AMAZON
RAINFOREST

DEAD SEA

ANTARCTICA
ANTARCTICA